ANTONIO ROSMINI:

INTRODUCTION TO HIS LIFE AND TEACHING

Antonio Rosmini:

Introduction to His Life and Teaching

by

Denis Cleary

**ROSMINI HOUSE
DURHAM**

ISBN 0 951 3211 6 1

Note

Preface

TO INTRODUCE a person's life and teaching is to invite others to experience and share the wonder of an existence not their own. The extent of the invitation is never easy to decide. In the case of Rosmini, I have become ever more aware, while writing this introduction, of a figure of immense intellectual and spiritual stature, but almost unknown outside Italian-speaking circles, who consistently unveils a profoundly satisfying meaning to so many aspects of reality. His immense output, his untiring application to his studies, his extensive correspondence, the care of his religious Institute and above all his dedication to the interior life cry out, even in a summary introduction, for fuller and more systematic illumination than I could hope to bring to the matter here. I have, therefore, contented myself with presenting Rosmini's basic tenets, and setting them out in a way which I hope will enable everyone to find something of interest in his work.

Each section of the introduction to his teaching points to conclusions reached by Rosmini in a particular field of study, and contains some indication of how he arrived at those conclusions. To this extent, individual sections can be read as separate units. Taken together, the sections support and corroborate one another while providing an overall picture of Rosmini's contribution to the history of his time and to the development of thought. But calling attention to part or whole of Rosmini's work is my only justification for this tentative effort to introduce him and make him better known.

Denis Cleary

Durham
March, 1992.

Contents

Chapter 1.

Rosmini's Life[1]

ANTONIO Rosmini-Serbati was born on March 24th, 1797, at Rovereto, a prosperous town in the Tyrol, then part of the Austro-Hungarian dominions in northern Italy. His father, Pier Modesto, was an upright, conservative head of a wealthy family that included Giovanna, Antonio's mother, a woman of great piety and sensitivity, Gioseffa Margherita, Rosmini's sister, about three years older than himself, and later Giuseppe, his younger brother. A warm relationship between Antonio and his sister, who would die as a Daughter of Charity of Canossa at the age of 39, was noticeably different from that between him and Giuseppe, whose unstable character was to cause his brother considerable concern later in life.

The great influences on the young Antonio were his mother, his bachelor uncle Ambrogio, a noted artist who also formed part of the Rosmini household, and Don Piero Orsi, a local priest who guided the adolescent's philosophical studies. But everyone in the household seems to have contributed to developing the extraordinary balance that was so marked a feature of Rosmini's life as a child and as a young man. It was in the family that he first experienced the practical Christianity of a closely knit community: Rosmini's nurse and his earliest tutor, for example, formed part of that 'community' until their death. Here, too, he felt the general aversion to the excesses of the French Revolution that remained with him all his life. The

[1] Cf. *Vita di Antonio Rosmini*, by a priest of the Institute of Charity, revised and updated by Guido Rossi, 2 vols., Rovereto, 1959; Claude Leetham, *Rosmini, Priest and Philosopher*, New York, 1982.

'domestic society', as he would later call it, also proved the perfect foil for the exuberant enthusiasm that marked Rosmini's early life.

It was typical of the civic spirit of the family that Rosmini's education should be entrusted for ten years to the public academy in Rovereto. Having learnt to read at home from the Bible and religious books, he began school as a seven-year old, completed the normal course, and simultaneously educated himself as a polymath in his uncle's library. There seems little doubt that at the age of sixteen, the foundations of immense erudition had been laid and that Rosmini had formulated for himself a rigorous method of study which precluded the waste of a single instant.[2] At the same time, he was genuinely popular with his peers.

Rosmini's last two years at school gave him the opportunity of a philosophical grounding which developed to an extraordinary extent in the additional classes held for himself and other youngsters of well-to-do families. He was able to write to a friend in 1816 defining philosophy as 'the great, first and fundamental study, the principle and key to all the others'.[3]

The young man's higher studies were completed in the theology and canon law faculties of the university of Padua, where he also studied medicine in some depth. His long-desired ordination to the priesthood took place in 1821, the

[2] Rosmini's use of time is one of the most striking external features of his life, and remains something of a mystery even today. His phenomenal literary output numbers more than 80 volumes on every aspect of philosophy and theology, and his edited correspondence (about two-thirds of all his letters, part of which form treatises on their own) runs to 13 volumes of about 700 pages each (*Epistolario completo*, vols I-XIII, Casale Monferrato 1887). By necessity a great traveller in northern and central Italy, he also founded a religious congregation, the Institute of Charity, was endlessly engaged in the great questions of the day, carried out his spiritual duties as priest and as director of hundreds of souls, and was noted for his hospitality.

[3] To Giovanni Fedrigotti at Vienna (EC, vol. 1, p. 157).

same year in which he gained clear insight into the principle or rule which was to govern all his future activity. To explain this, however, we have to retrace our steps a little.

Until this moment, Rosmini's life although noted for application to studies, was also remarkable for spiritual intensity and a desire to love God and his neighbour which had found an outlet in immense projects characteristic of his great breadth of mind. His attempt to found a publishing house destined to produce a Christian *Encyclopedia* rivalling the French Encyclopedia of the previous century was wholly consistent with his intellectual and spiritual aims. His projected *Society of Friends*[4] was another massive, world-wide undertaking that he had at heart. More practical was his attempt to found in the Rosmini home a library that would serve the intelligentsia of the whole town.

But all these plans came to nothing, and Rosmini was compelled to ask himself whether they sprang more from his subjective desire to do good than from a desire to do the will of God. He concluded that true wisdom dictated immediate attention to his own holiness, but acceptance of good works only when it became obvious that this was the will of God for him. He called this his 'principle of passivity', a principle that would simultaneously offer him the opportunity of uniting a deeply prayerful life with readiness to undertake whatever work for his neighbour should be placed in his path by Providence.

From 1821 to 1828 Rosmini was led by this principle to devote himself to study first at Rovereto where he had inherited the considerable family fortune on the death of his father, and later at Milan where he was able to take advantage of the facilities provided by the great libraries in the city. Here he prepared his first great philosophical work on the origin of ideas, and undertook a thorough examination of the rules of religious orders throughout the history of the Church.

[4] The name could be misleading in an English-speaking context. No reference is intended to Quaker assemblies.

In 1823, Rosmini went for the first time to Rome where he met Cardinal Castiglione, later Pius VIII, and Cardinal Cappellari, later Gregory XVI, and could have embarked on a prestigious ecclesiastical career. But his most enduring memory of the journey was the encouragement he received from Pius VII to persevere in his philosophical studies. The Pope's words were an assurance for Rosmini that these studies truly formed part of God's calling for him, and he returned to the north of Italy determined to pursue them. At the time of his third visit to Rome (1830) he was already well known in Italian literary circles. Manzoni[5] and Tommaseo[6] in particular were outstanding friends of his.

Rosmini's study of religious life in the Church had been prompted in part by an invitation, which he did not pursue, to collaborate in the foundation of a religious order of men. This was intended to correspond to one for women instituted by Maddalena di Canossa, a formidable and holy descendant of the redoubtable Matilda di Canossa. But his work did come to fruition in a practical sense when he took the opportunity provided by Providence to leave the comfort of Milan in 1828 for an isolated sanctuary at Domodossola, a singularly unattractive Piedmontese town near the Italo-Swiss border. Here in solitude he wrote *Constitutiones Societatis a Caritate nuncupatae*[7] a remarkable work that incorporated his own 'principle of passivity'[8] and his intimate knowledge of the

[5] The author of Italy's most famous novel, *I Promessi Sposi* (*The Betrothed*).

[6] The great lexicographer, compiler of *Dizionario della lingua italiana* (Turin 1865), 'perhaps the only truly worthy monument to Italian unity' (Gianfranco Folena in his Introduction to the Dictionary, 1977).

[7] [London, 1875]; translated as *The Constitutions of the Society of Charity*, Durham, 1988.

[8] Rosmini's basic teaching on the spiritual life will be found in his *Maxims of Perfection* [1830] (Cf. *Rosminian Spirituality*, An Anthology, Cardiff, 1977, pp. 171-199 However, translations of *MP* in the present work are made directly from the critical edition, Stresa, 1981).

experience provided by the continuing development of religious life throughout the history of the Church. The *Institute of Charity*, which grew as companions joined Rosmini at Domodossola and which he governed until his death, looks to these *Constitutions* as the written basis of its spiritual existence.

In 1830 Rosmini, already well known through various philosophical writings of an occasional nature, principally on happiness and the unity of education, published his *Nuovo saggio sull'origine delle idee*.[9] This was followed by a torrent of philosophical and theological works which continued in full flood until his death in 1855.

The last twenty-five years of Rosmini's life were marked not only by his literary activity and the government of his religious Institute, but by a crescendo of opposition from political and religious adversaries. The intense criticism to which he was subject made itself felt in the difficulties raised about the pontifical approval of his Congregation, in the problems caused for him by the Austrian government, in the furious polemic aroused by his *Trattato sulla coscienza morale*,[10] and in his rejection by Pius IX, at whose request Rosmini had accompanied the Pope on his flight from Rome to Gaeta after the assassination in 1848 of Pellegrino Rossi, prime minister of the Papal States.

During this period opinions about Rosmini varied from those expressed in a quasi-epitaph written by Gregory XVI in the document of approbation of the *Institute of Charity*,[11] to the accusations levelled at him by his opponents. For the Pope, he was a priest 'endowed with lofty and surpassing genius,

[9] *Nuovo Saggio sull'origine delle idee* [1830], 3 vols., *EN*, Rome, 1934; second volume translated under the title, *The Origin of Thought*, Durham 1988, third volume translated as *Certainty*, Durham 1992.

[10] [1839], translated under the title *Conscience*, Durham, 1989.

[11] *In Sublimi* [1839], published with an accompanying Italian translation, Turin 1894.

adorned with extraordinary gifts of soul, renowned in the highest degree for his knowledge of things human and divine, distinguished for his remarkable piety';[12] for others he was 'a hypocrite, disloyal, a Jansenist wolf, a teacher of hellish doctrine, a traitor to the Church, and of such human and diabolical evil that it would be difficult to go further.'[13]

To the world at large, Rosmini remained a centre of controversy until his death in 1855, and for many years afterwards. His devotion to the Church brought him to accept without difficulty, but with immense pain, the listing (1849) of his *Delle cinque piaghe della santa chiesa*[14] and his *La Costituzione civile secondo la giustizia sociale*[15] on the *Index of Forbidden Books*.[16] On the other hand an extensive examination by a papal commission instituted for the purpose declared in 1854, one year before Rosmini's death, that all his works should be dismissed without censure of any kind.[17]

While the controversy raged, Rosmini continued to study and write. Almost his last published work was *Sulla libertà dell'insegnamento*[18] (*Freedom to Teach*) written in defence of threatened liberty in the schools of Piedmont. But the most interesting and important of his last writings remained unpublished at his death. These will be detailed in the examination to which we must now subject the major propositions of what Rosmini called 'the system of truth'.

---

[12] *Ibid.* p. 78.

[13] The language, although fairly typical of that used in philosophical controversy at the time, does no honour to its author.

[14] *Delle cinque piaghe della santa Chiesa* [1846], translated under the title, *The Five Wounds of the Church*, Durham, 1986.

[15] *La Costituzione civile secondo la giustizia sociale* [1848], Milan, 1952.

[16] *see* chap. 3, 'Controversies'.

[17] *see* chap. 3, 'Controversies', for a brief description of posthumous difficulties.

[18] [1854], L'Aquila-Rome, 1987.

Chapter 2.

Rosmini's Philosophical Teaching

1. The problem of knowledge[19]

Reflection

ROSMINI had begun his philosophical journey in a spirit of optimism, but by 1826 realised that there was no hope of progress in the various divisions of philosophy until its source of unity had been thoroughly investigated. In his eyes the dignity of philosophy had been seriously compromised by the basically sceptical work of his immediate predecessors in Germany (Kant, Hegel, Fichte and Schelling), and by British empiricism (represented in particular by Locke, Hume and Reid). At the same time, Rosmini was glad to concede that the problems raised in the 18th century had been of great assistance in concentrating the mind on the fundamental difficulties connected with the theory of knowledge.

Rosmini takes a fact of observation for his starting point in considering the problem of knowledge: human beings can and do reflect on what they know. Reflection, the characteristic activity that separates humans from all other beings in the world, enables us to seek reasons for things and events. We want to know why things happen. But the reasons we immediately discover lead us to more universal explanations as we pass from one stage of enquiry to another. What we know at one level is included in the next level that we attain. Our knowledge, says Rosmini, is like a pyramid:

[19] Cf. especially *NS* (in English, *OT* and *Certainty*); *Logica* [1853], CrE, Stresa, 1984; *Rinnovamento della filosofia in Italia* [1836], *EN*, Milan, 1941; *Introduzione alla filosofia* [1850], CrE, Stresa, 1979.

Its base is huge, and formed of the innumerable, particular truths we know. These truths are the stones at the bottom of the pyramid. Above them runs another level of more universal truths, fewer in number but embracing all that will be developed at the lowest level. We go up from level to level ... until we arrive at the top of the pyramid where the multiplicity of stones merges in the unity of a single block which extends potentially to all that lies beneath it.[20]

Philosophy begins when we sense the need to ascend with our reflection to the highest, most universal level of reflection where we can discover the ultimate reasons of human knowledge.

The difficulties of the ascent are acknowledged by Rosmini who foresees that it can be undertaken satisfactorily only by those courageous enough to 'dare philosophically' for the love of truth, and to abandon dispassionately, but perhaps not without pain, every private or historical opinion that contradicts the truth they come to know on their journey.

Philosophy does not end, however, when the summit of knowledge has been attained. The search for the tranquillity and quiet of mind provided by the unifying factor in knowledge is replaced by a desire to see how new knowledge derives from the potentiality of fundamental knowledge, and how new problems take their place within the broad spectrum of what is known.

Thus the value of philosophy according to Rosmini depends upon respect for reason as a means for attaining the truth. He rejects any understanding of philosophy which reduces it to a simple analysis of language (positivism), to a subjective search for unattainable truth (scepticism), or to the expression of an individual existence caught up in some unforeseeable journey towards annihilation (existentialism).

The origin of ideas

Reflection, the very heart of philosophy, depends upon

[20] *IF*, no. 8.

judgments, and judgments depend upon uniting a predicate to a subject. We say, for example, 'This stone is white.' But the characteristic of a predicate is that it always contains an element of *universality*. I cannot say: 'This stone is white' without first knowing what 'whiteness' is. But whiteness is universal: it can be used, and is used, to enable me to affirm that an innumerable series of things are white. The problem that other philosophers saw, but did not succeed in resolving, is concerned with the origin of the universality implicit in every predicate: how does this universality arrive in the mind?

Critical philosophy — the German school dependent upon Kant — saw that universality could not be explained by dependence upon sense. But these philosophers, in establishing forms or categories of the mind as the source of the universal content of idea, admitted more than was necessary on the one hand, and on the other prepared the ground for total scepticism. Some innate element was necessary to the mind, but not categories or subjective forms.

British empiricism took a totally different path by denying the existence of any idea; its inability to distinguish clearly between sense and judgment, and its refusal to grant anything to the intellect other than the sensations on which the mind draws for knowledge, led to a complete impasse in the face of the difficulty raised by the passage from particulars to universals. The almost inevitable result was the rejection of universals and the propagation of materialism.

Both Critical philosophy and British empiricism, however, had concentrated their attention on the nature of the human, intellective faculty. Rosmini saw that another approach was needed. An indisputable fact of knowledge, not an interpretation of the working intellect, was to be the basis on which progress could be made.

> I begin with a simple, very obvious fact ... we think of being in a general way. This fact, no matter how we explain it, cannot be called into doubt ...To deny that we can direct our attention to being as common to all things while ignoring or rather abstracting from all their other qualities, contradicts

what is attested by ordinary observation of our own actions; it would mean contradicting common sense and violating ordinary speech. ... This fact is so obvious that to mention it would be sufficient, if it were not for the doubt prevalent in modern thinking. Yet it is the foundation of the origin of ideas.[21]

In other words, the least that we can say of anything while maintaining it as an object of thought is: 'This (whatever it may be) *is* something'.

To think being in a general way means that we have the idea of being in general, or at least presupposes that we have it; without the idea of being, we cannot think being. Our task, therefore, is to identify the origin of this idea. But if we are to discover its source, we must first examine its nature and character[22]

Rosmini's analysis of the idea of being indicates the presence in it of the following characteristics: possibility, because this idea provides the possibility of all thought; objectivity, because it is immune to change by the thinking subject; simplicity, because it lacks extension; unity, because it is the intelligibility of all that is; universality, because every other idea must be in some way a qualification of the idea of being; necessity, because it cannot be thought of as not being; indetermination, because it stands as the basis of all ideas and cannot therefore be determined in any way.

None of these things can be explained by Locke's abstraction and reflection, nor by Kant's immanent forms and categories. The only 'ideology' corresponding to the unescapable fact of the understanding of being as common to every human intellect is the innate presence to the human intelligence of the idea of being. This idea is the form of the intelligence because it provides the first act rendering the human being intelligent; it is innate, but a presence which is not confused with ourselves; it is intuited as a light of the mind. It is not an immanent, subjective form; it is a transcendent,

[21] *OT*, no. 398.
[22] *Ibid*., no. 399.

objective form. Like a light, it illuminates without becoming the eyes of the beholder; it is not the seer, but what is seen; it is the known object which enlightens the knowing subject.

But the subject furnished with this objective, indeterminate form of being also knows various modes of being as a result of its sense experience. Rosmini does not neglect this equally obvious fact in human existence. For him, sensation provides the determinations which in their turn are beheld within the light emanating from the idea of being. Thus the determinations *are* something, although they do not alter the light itself in which they are seen.

All this takes place within the unity of the human subject, the meeting-place of the two elements, idea and sense-experience. Rosmini appeals

> to the unity of the human being, to the simplicity of the human spirit. 'Myself', the principle which knows that something is a being, is the same principle which experiences action within itself, because feeling is an action of being'.[23]

This capacity for uniting being and feeling, the ideal and the real, in an act of knowledge is what Rosmini calls 'reason'. The first act with which the mind reasons is intellective perception or apprehension, the basic judgment in which all others are grounded.

At this point, it becomes necessary for Rosmini to analyse the material part of knowledge and uncover its origin. Observation leads us to two kinds of feeling: internal and external. Internal feelings are characterised by total lack of extension — my pains and pleasures, for example, have no shape or external content whatsoever, and cannot be experienced except by the one who perceives them; external feelings have some content (shape, colour, smell, etc.,) which can be experienced by many people, although never in exactly the same way. Internal feelings are dependent upon the perception of *my* body — they lack extension because I first feel this body of mine as a whole, without the limits caused by the presence of other bodies, or

[23] *Psicologia* [1846-1848], no. 264, CrE, Stresa, 1988.

even of my own body acting upon itself in the way any other body would; external feelings depend upon the perception of other bodies, including that of my own when it acts as a foreign body. 'Body' is energy exerted by one element of the animal upon the 'anima', the other constituent of animal; it produces a basic 'fundamental feeling' of which all other feelings are modifications. Internal sensations (subjective feelings) are direct modifications of the fundamental feeling; external sensations (extrasubjective feelings) are modifications of the fundamental feeling produced by the indirect action of bodies, including the subject's own. All sensations constitute the material part of our knowledge.

Every idea, therefore, except the idea of being, is composed of a formal and a material element. The formal element is the idea of being itself, the light which illumines every human being, without itself suffering any action from that which it illumines; the material element is given by 'body', a force which acts on a principle suitable for perceiving it. The union of these two elements is found in the human being, and explains the problem of the origin and nature of ideas without sacrificing the intelligibility of being (the sceptical defect inherent in Hume's philosophy) or the real existence of the world (the idealistic defect of Berkeley's system).

Certainty

We are well placed now to deal with the problem of certainty. It is not a difficulty associated with the objective world of knowledge, but with the human subject's *re*action to what it knows. Being is being: nothing more can be said about knowledge in the last analysis than that. We can, however, either allow ourselves to be persuaded by what we know, or refuse to posit the energy of spirit that produces persuasion. When we do unfold this energy consistently and firmly in accord with what we know we are said to be certain. 'Certainty', says Rosmini, 'is a firm and reasonable persuasion that conforms to the truth'. In other words, we not only know something to be true, to be what it is, but we are also firmly persuaded that it is what we know it to be, and have a reason for our persuasion. The criterion is always the idea of being, which precedes every judgment and all reasoning and is therefore inviolate. As the criterion it is the truth of things because in it they are presented to us as they are. Error is present in our spirit when we declare something to be what it is not or deny that something is what it is. And precisely because error alters the being of things, formal error will not be found rooted in the intellect nor in the senses nor in involuntary reflection. Such error begins with the will, the only human faculty capable of drawing the reason to invent what it does not see, or to deny what it sees. Under pressure from the will, the reason will falsely affirm that being is not, or deny that being is.

2. The human person[24]

Having established the basis of a theory of knowledge through consideration of the essential, known object (being), Rosmini's next step is to consider the nature of the human subject. This, in turn, requires an analysis of the constitutive animal and intellective elements of the human being as a means towards presenting an adequate anthropology and psychology of human nature.

At this point, reading Rosmini becomes both difficult and extremely rewarding for the modern mind. The difficulties arise from our habit, evident especially in scientific studies, of giving almost total attention to quantifiable, sense phenomena. In psychology, for example, we find ourselves dealing with *psycho*logical phenomena without attempting to examine the problem of the existence and nature of '*psyche*'; we think about the characteristics of '*person*ality' without reference to any underlying *person*. These mental habits are so

[24] Cf. especially *Antropologia in servigio delle scienze morali* [1838] CrE, Stresa, 1981, translated as *Anthroplogy as an Aid to Moral Science*, Durham, 1992; *Psicologia* [1846-48], CrE, Stresa, 1988.

ingrained that we tend to categorise all thinking in this way. The result, when we find ourselves face to face with reasoning like Rosmini's, which will not conform to our own intellectual activity, is a genuine sense of disorientation. We seem to move in an unreal world, and we are left with profound misgivings.

At the same time, the phenomenological world is essentially incapable of offering any lasting, satisfactory solution to the fundamental problems arising from our perceived status as human beings. 'A bundle of sensations', as human beings have often been described, is too flippant a way of dismissing the problems involved in self-examination and analysis. Rosmini, while requiring us to look at and observe adequately the whole of nature, draws us beyond the phenomena to what sustains them, and in particular to the human person, the individual, the unquantifiable mystery which each one of us senses himself to be. Rosmini is determined to present both the phenomena and their underlying explanation.

Two elements are to hand as undeniable factors of our experience; *being* as intuited and known, the basis of all knowledge, and *feeling*, the foundation of human subjectivity. Rosmini's theory of knowledge deals principally with intuited *being*, and his anthropology and psychology with the nature of animal and intellective *feeling*.

Animal feeling, which we so often take as solely phenomenological, has its place for Rosmini amongst the elements which provide the final explanation of human phenomena. On the basis of observation which, he insists, has to take account both of order in feeling and of our conscious individuality, we arrive at a first feeling, the principle and subject of all other feelings, that is, at a feeling without which other feelings cannot exist. This feeling, as first act, is life; it is a substantial, fundamental feeling; it is what we call properly 'soul' (in our present case 'the animal aspect of the soul'). The soul provides a basis for all other feelings that occur within us, and posits the individuality which establishes each of us with our own incommunicability.

> The soul is an originating, stable feeling, the unique principle
> and unique subject of all other feelings and human activities[25]

But the feeling which properly speaking constitutes the substance of the soul[26] is made up of two distinct, but inseparable elements. On the one hand, we find a simple, immaterial, sentient principle; on the other the extended, felt term:

> That which is felt and that which feels make up a single feeling
> which, as the first and fundamental feeling, is a unique entity.[27]

However, because the union between sentient principle and felt term is that proper to form and matter, and not that of two individual substances, the feeling principle as form (and consequently as that which provides the intelligibility and nomenclature of feeling) is given the name 'soul'

The soul is tied to its own body by the bond of uniform, indeterminate, shapeless feeling. This is the subjective feeling with which the animal feels itself and which a human being at a given level of consciousness calls 'myself'. Within this general feeling, that which feels experiences all the modifications taking place in the energy called its own body. Such modifications can be provoked either by the feeling principle itself or by external agents. Sensations springing from the subject-agent produce subjective modifications in the fundamental feeling; sensations coming from the action of bodies other than one's own, or from one's own as from a foreign body, produce what Rosmini calls 'extrasubjective' phenomena.

This fundamental corporeal feeling and its modifications throw light on the animal element of the soul. The rational element is discovered as we meditate on 'myself'. Careful attention to 'myself' reveals the presence in the human being of purely spiritual feelings, that is, of feelings which terminate neither in extension nor in matter of any kind whatsoever.

Chief amongst these feelings is that encompassed by the

---

[25] *Psicologia*, CrE, t. 1, no. 129.

[26] Cf. *ibid*, no. 81.

[27] *Ibid*, no. 250.

very word 'myself' which describes our essential self, and indicates something unique, separate and altogether distinct from everything else. The incorporeal, immaterial feeling to which we refer, whose reality cannot be denied despite its total lack of extension and its imperviousness to space of any kind, is spiritual of its nature. Its origin is found in the union existing between the knowing subject and the idea of being.

'Myself', therefore, is a single subject with two terms, the idea of being and the body I call my own. 'Myself' is not two subjects but one, which undertakes simultaneously animal and rational activities. I who understand, feel, and I who feel, understand.

This is possible, according to Rosmini, because the intelligent and animal aspects of soul both have an outreach to *being*. The intelligent part of 'myself' terminates in being as understood; the animal part of 'myself' terminates in being as felt. The single subject uniting in itself the fundamental, corporeal principle and the vision of being becomes a rational principle which sees the fundamental feeling in the light of the being it intuits. When this takes place a new human nature is realised.

> This primitive and fundamental perception of all that is felt (principle and term) is the marriage-bed, as it were, where that which is real (the animal-spiritual feeling) and the essence intuited in the idea of being form a single thing; and this single reality is a new human being.[28]

The human being, therefore, is composed of animality, of reason (intelligence and will), and of a principle common to animality and reason, the human subject. This subject is the supreme principle, the root and the fount of real existence and activity in the human being. As supreme, it is also the human person.

At this point, Rosmini is able to distinguish between the action of the individual as person, and as human being. Only one principle is supreme in the human being; in so far as action is directed by this principle, the human being acts as a person.

---

[28] *Ibid*, no. 261.

But there are within the human being multiple sources of activity (feelings, desires, instincts), each rooted in its own proper principle. If any of these principles acts independently of the supreme principle, consequent acts of such a principle are natural, but not personal. And it is a fact that there are many branches of human activity which reach very high levels of perfection without involving personal activity. The development of modern science, for example, does not necessarily entail greater moral perfection in human beings; knowledge is not always wisdom; 'progress' is not synonymous with 'civilisation' when the human person, the only principle capable of involving in progress the total human being, has been set aside. When the supreme principle acts in its fullness, it has at its command the use of those first acts which make up the primary elements of the human being.

The primary activities of the soul according to Rosmini, who goes on to analyse human activity in great detail, are constituted by the powers of intellect and will, sense and instinct, and reason. Sense is passive in so far as it is limited to receiving some modification from an agent (body); intellect is receptive in so far as it receives the idea of being without confusion between itself and this idea. Instinct and will are the reactive powers which spring from the passivity and receptivity of sense and intellect. Instinct, which is active, can change both itself and the term on which it operates; the will, which is also active, cannot change its term, the ideas (towards which it is receptive), but can change its choice of activity relative to those ideas by acknowledging or refusing to acknowledge them for what they are.

Rosmini's detailed analysis of the activity of these powers is devoted to clarifying their different modes of being. His pages on the manner in which sense and instinct operate are highly original. In particular, he shows at length that animal instinct is far more versatile than we usually imagine, and dependent not upon any use of intelligence, but to a great extent on laws of harmony found within purely animal reality and with nature at large. Nevertheless, in the human being the unity of intelligence and sense within an individual is beneficial and necessary to human and personal well-being. Although ideal being is given *in toto* to the human intelligence, and is thus simple and indivisible, it does not furnish the mind with anything real (I cannot produce anything, for example, simply by thinking about it). On the other hand, being as seen by the mind is effectively participated by the human subject through the subject's real power of feeling, but in a limited, piecemeal way only.

3. Person and morality[29]

Morality

For Rosmini, the human being is a knowing and feeling subject whose will, as supreme principle of activity, provides the basis of the incommunicable individuality that constitutes each human creature as a person. Morality is concerned with personal activity.

This sets morality aside from all lesser human activities which, although capable of perfecting human beings in particular ways, do not touch their inner core as persons. A good pianist, for example, is not necessarily a good person; a good linguist is not necessarily a good person. Perfection at the level of music or languages is quite different from the perfection that lies within the capacities of persons as persons. What human beings do as pianists or linguists may well be efficacious in the limited spheres of music and linguistics; but what they do as 'person' affects their whole being — and it is here that morality holds sway.

Morality possesses a second characteristic which further sets it apart from other human activities. It commands and obliges

[29] Cf. especially *Principi della scienza morale* [1831], *EN*, Milan, 1941, translated as *Principles of Ethics*, Durham, 1988, and *Storia comparativa e critica dei sistemi intorno al principio della Morale* [1837], *EN*, Milan, 1941.

without compromise or promise. Although it brings human beings to perfection as persons, it does not present this perfection in the guise of something subjectively beneficial (although morality in one sense will always be beneficial); it offers only obligation which binds the person irrespective of any effect it may produce in him. Morality, therefore, determines human actions with the force of obligation.

The first moral law

Ethics, the branch of knowledge dealing with morality, is as different from other branches of knowledge as its subject, morality, is different from other human activities:

> ... ethics, with its absolute exigency, has its own place superior to every other branch of philosophy. Its object is not humanity or some other finite nature, but eternal, unshakeable truths requiring unconditional respect and obedience. Such truths are independent of reasons extrinsic to themselves; the respect we owe them is based upon a simple, irrefutable, evident reason shining in them and impervious to exceptions, ignorance, contradiction and violence of any sort.[30]

The purpose of ethics, therefore, is in the first place to indicate a law that self-evidently imposes its obligation upon willed human actions. For Rosmini, this law is the ultimate expression to which all obligatory laws can be reduced, namely, 'acknowledge (recognise) what you know for what you know it to be'. Not to acknowledge what is known for what it is known to be is self-evidently contradictory and an interior lie. Such an action denies the known truth, sets the lying subject against the order of being, and overthrows the internal harmony of which the human subject is capable.

It is clear that this final expression of moral law is itself dependent solely upon the notion of being, which is present to the human mind that it forms. The innate light of the intellect becomes, from this point of view, the notion which we use to produce all moral judgments. As such this light is itself the first moral law. Relative to the light of being, the law states: 'In

[30] *Preface to the works of moral philosophy*, in *PE*, 9.

what you do, follow the light of reason'. The command is not concerned with reason in the first place, but with the *light* of reason. Only the light itself is objective and immune from error; reason, a subjective activity, can and does err.

Important consequences result from the relationship between morality and the first moral law and the light of being. Because the light of being is innate, human beings begin their existence rooted in morality and in potential moral obligation. This obligation may later be denied at the subjective level through refusal to acknowledge what is known for what it is, but it cannot be manipulated objectively: what is, cannot not be. In addition the law, which is common to all individuals irrespective of their race, sex, nation, culture or religion, binds everyone without exception.

Rosmini's clear distinction between the knowing subject and the known object opens a way between the present extremes of ethical theory. The limitation and mutability of the human subject provide for the possibility of moral error on the part of the subject; the necessity and immutability of the idea of being furnish morality with its undeniable sense of obligation. Obscuring this distinction has led on the one hand to theories of human autonomy in which attributes proper to the object have been predicated of the subject; and on the other, to theories of mutability in the moral law because attributes of the subject have been predicated about the object.

Moral good

That which is, is good, that is to say, it is desirable. But it may be desirable in itself according to its place in the whole economy of being or it may be desirable for me, the subject, because of the satisfaction it brings me when I possess it. In order to conform with the moral law, I must acknowledge things not in so far as they are good for me, the human subject, but in so far as they take their place in the order of being. In this way, I bring myself to harmonise with objective being as such; I do not bring being to harmonise with me, and thus set myself up as the arbiter of being. My final good, the moral good springing from the first moral law, comes about through the acknowledgement of what is. By this acknowledgement, I take my place willingly in the order of being. Acknowledging in practice what is for what I know it to be, I become one, by my own action, with all that is. As 'person', the human subject is the power for affirming the whole of being as the subject apprehends it.[31]

Such practical acknowledgement does not and cannot depend upon our capacity for recognising the place of every individual entity in the order of being. But a distinction can and is made easily as we develop and come to see that a major difference exists between persons and things. This difference depends on what I come to know about myself first of all, and the things that surround me. Knowing what I am, I then come to know other persons as possessing the same grade of being as myself, and thus as worthy of the same respect as myself. In particular, I see that every person is to be treated as an end, not as a means. The innate dignity conferred on human beings by their very existence as intelligent beings becomes an absolute, inviolable right to be recognised wherever I find it.

What is said about human beings is *a fortiori* true of the Absolute which confers upon them the light of being. All moral good is found in the acknowledgement of the classes of intelligent beings at their level of relationship with Absolute Being; no moral good can be found outside the ranks of intelligent beings.

The practical acknowledgement of moral good

The practical acknowledgement of moral good depends upon an act of will by which we esteem beings for what they are. This esteem lies at the root of every other action that I posit relative to what I know. If, for example, I accept in practice my parents for what they are, I will be grateful for the life they have given me. I will esteem them as my lifegivers,

---

[31] Cf. *The Essence of Right*, 143 (Durham 1992, vol. 1 of the translation of *Filosofia del diritto*, Intra 1865)

irrespective of other relationships they may have with me. On the other hand, I may refuse to recognise in practice that another man or woman is my friend's husband/wife, and consider myself entitled to establish an intimate relationship with him or her. Through my esteem or lack of it, I engender within myself the act of love or hatred that turns me towards or against what I know. When I do this freely, I decide of my own accord to place myself in a moral or immoral state; I do good or I do evil.

Conscience[32]

'Conscience is a judgment by which we come to know the moral value of our action.' Rosmini's definition shows immediately the nature and place of conscience in the moral sphere. Conscience, although it may be occasioned by a feeling of guilt, is not itself a feeling, but a reflection upon the moral worth of our action or actions. As a reflection, conscience does not cause but evaluates the morality of what we have done or are about to do. Consequently, it is not and cannot be the fundamental source of morality in our lives. It is at most a secondary source and as such is itself subject to the first moral law. In other words, my evaluation of the moral worth of my actions must be governed by the need to recognise those actions for what they are. If I willingly blind myself to their morality or immorality by making a false judgment about them, my conscience itself is flawed and therefore immoral.

The clarity of such fundamental statements throws brilliant light upon moral problems connected with conscience. In particular it shows that conscience cannot be given an absolute place in morality. It is not correct to say that we must always follow our conscience. If the judgment by which conscience comes about is itself deliberately misleading and immoral, it cannot be a safe guide to the moral worth of my action: I end by telling myself that what is right is wrong, or that what is

[32] Cf. especially *Trattato della coscienza morale* [1839], *EN*, 1954, translated under the title: *Conscience*, Durham, 1990.

wrong is right. In either case I will be deceiving myself. Conscience is an adequate guide only when it informs me uprightly of the morality of an action by judging according to the objective order of being.

On the other hand, I cannot disregard the judgment of conscience by acting contrary to conscience. In this sense, conscience is a negative absolute and I may never act against it. The dilemma in such a case is resolved only by a decision to correct the conscience which, as false, always betrays itself through the inevitable unease provoked interiorly as conscience clashes with the light of being.

> There is a light in the human being, and a light that is the human being: the light in the human being is ... the law of truth; the light that is the human being is an upright conscience ... we become light when we share in the law of truth by means of an upright conscience in conformity with truth.[33]

Rosmini's definition of conscience opens the way to resolving other problems in this field. First, it allows us to see clearly that it is possible for morality and immorality to exist in the human subject irrespective of reflection. Although knowledge is indeed required by a subject for moral action, this knowledge is concerned essentially with the object I must *ac*knowledge; it is not necessarily knowledge of my state as the person positing the moral action. In other words, morality is present in the subject by means of an act of will which *ac*knowledges or *re*cognises what is known directly without any reflection; only then can our conscience, that is, our judgment about the moral state resulting from our action, come into play.

Second, we can reject all pseudo-problems connected with what is erroneously called 'doubtful' conscience. Doubt about the morality of an action shows that in fact conscience has not yet been formed; in the case of doubt, our judgment remains suspended. Problems arise, but they are concerned with the *formation* of conscience, not with difficulties about whether we should follow conscience. In other words, we need to

[33] *Conscience*, 427.

know how to reach conclusions of conscience in cases of doubt. Rosmini deals at length with the laws governing such matters.

Third, Rosmini's definition offers a platform from which to view the varying development of conscience in different people, at different ages in the same person, in nations at different stages of growth, and in the light provided by new problems arising from the advance of science and technology.

> No modern teaching about morals ... can be accepted unless it is a legitimate *conclusion* from earlier principles as old as ... reason. The conclusion must be tied to these eternal principles ... What matters is the final connection with the irrefutable principles. Granted this connection, the *conclusion*, resulting from new circumstances, new positive laws, and new relationships discovered by the mind, can be as *new* as we wish. In short, it is drawn from a *new level of reflection*.[34]

4. Person and society

Rosmini is not content with providing a description of the human being which is limited to the essential characteristics of person. These incommunicable elements depend for their growth and development on the reaction between persons within a social context, and it is this context which forms the frame of reference for the other branches of philosophy to which Rosmini applied himself. In particular he devoted his attention to the philosophy of education, of human rights, of politics and art. We shall deal with each of them in turn.

It will be helpful, however, if we first consider Rosmini's general description of society.[35] For him, a society can never be merely an external organisation. It is rather a group of

---

[34] *Conscience*, 213.

[35] Cf. especially *La società e il suo fine* (Society and its End) [1837], Milan, 1858; *Della sommaria cagione per la quale stanno o si rovinano le umane società* (The Summary Cause explaining the Preservation or Self-destruction of Human Societies) [1837], Venice, 1945

persons who will to join together for the attainment of a common end. The key to proper understanding of any society lies in the willed desire of the members to be together for the sake of reaching a goal that would either be impossible or difficult to achieve otherwise. This willed desire may be onto-logically irrevocable, as in the case of marriage, or revocable, as in the case of societies which may be dissolved with the members' consent, but in every society some act of will is needed for constituting the corporate body. Without this act of will, the external apparatus of society is a delusion.

5. Person and education[36]

Rosmini's distinction between the perfection of person and the perfection of human nature[37] is crucial to an understanding of his approach to the philosophy of education. Although nature can and does develop within the context of society, such development is not always accompanied by growth at a personal level. A perfectly competent astrophysicist, carpenter or secretary may be a moral misery to self and others; from a personal point of view, even the skills in use at the level of human nature may be employed evilly and disastrously.

Education is valid for Rosmini, therefore, only if it cultivates the whole person, and imparts instruction in such a way that the elements of human nature are developed in harmony with and subject to the requirements of the person. The aim of education, and its fount of unity, is the perfection of the person, the only source capable of ensuring an organic, global and harmonious development within the human being. At the same time, the human person tends to God as his ultimate end. In this sense, education goes beyond the limitations of the

---

[36] Cf. especially *Saggio sull'unità dell'educazione* (Essay on the Unity of Education) [1826], *Della libertà d'insegnamento* (Freedom to Teach) [1854], *Del principio supremo del metodo* (The Supreme Principle of Method) [1857], all of which may be found in *Scritti vari di metodo e di pedagogia*, Turin, 1883.

[37] Cf. p. 16.

human person by directing the person to God. In other words, no system of education is valid without its being at least implicitly religious. Education is intended to facilitate the growth of harmony in a person, and to aid the referral of the person to the end for which he exists.

The material content of education consists in teaching the means by which the end may be achieved. These means gravitate around three objects: God, the human being, and nature. The first is studied in theology, the second by means of history, philosophy and the humanities, and the third under the general title of natural sciences.

Rosmini examines the second area of education in some detail. For him, history includes literature, the history of philosophy and one's native language as well as the account of previous events in universal, national and regional fields. Considered from this point of view, history enables us to understand something of human effort through the centuries, with its successes and failures. But this in turn depends upon a valid criterion, provided by philosophy, for measuring progress and failure.

The teaching of natural sciences is not explicitly considered by Rosmini in any single work, but he says sufficient in passing to show that mathematics is of primary importance for the appraisal of method, that observation is absolutely necessary to prevent us from attempting — disastrously — to dictate laws to nature rather than receive them from nature, and that every progress in this field is to be welcomed when it goes hand in hand with personal development.

Two considerations must be kept in mind, therefore, if the advantages of true education are to be realised. First, the knowledge taught, although governed by rules in its own field, must be finally subordinated to the end comprised by the person; second, one or more subjects must not dominate to the extent of preventing the harmonious development of all that is needed to attain the end, that is, the growth of the human person.

Consideration of what is taught must be accompanied in the philosophy of education by an examination of the human faculties with which the person who learns grasps what is put before him. The human being is the living material on which the educator has to work. The teacher's effort will produce maximum good when his method succeeds in uniting harmoniously the senses, intellect and will of the students so that together these faculties collaborate in obtaining the perfection of the person who is the subject of education. The teacher uses this supreme principle of method in his work by leading the pupils from the known to the unknown, from the general to the particular, by drawing attention to what is common in the many particulars which we experience. This is in fact the way our instinct for education expresses itself. No one in their senses will say to a child: 'Look at the lovely carnations' before saying: 'Look at the lovely flowers'. In other words, and as far as possible, the particular will never be named before the more universal.

Such a method does not entail its rigid application to every pupil. It would be, says Rosmini, 'a sad, unreasonable approach which requires that everyone be educated like all the others'. Often the pupil's distaste for work is indicative of the teacher's lack of skill in this respect rather than incapacity on the part of the students. If those who learn are the living material of education, teachers are the living instruments and as such constitute the only essential elements in adequate education. Method, reforms in education and resources of every kind will be valueless without good teachers. At the same time, educators of 'great charity, sacrifice and ability' are capable of transforming impossible situations: 'Give me good teachers, and even schools poorly constituted and divided will be good'.[38]

Teachers therefore must be people of broad sympathies who know how to combine clear exposition with profound instruction, to show coherence between what they teach and

[38] *Logica*, no. 1033.

how they live, and to offer education serenely and firmly, with constant attention to the heart and will of the pupil, as well as to their understanding: 'the heart should feel, and life should make clear, what the intellect has grasped'.[39]

Rosmini, when speaking of teachers, does not direct his attention only to what we may call professional educators. Above all, he refers to parents whose instinct for educating their children will be needed long before formal teaching is required. The life instinct and the sensuous instinct, the awakening of intelligence, and language, all introduce the child into new worlds which can only be supervised by the parents and the immediate family of the child. At each level of development, children will have to receive the kind of education that can be adapted to *their* rules. It would be wrong to force growth at any of these stages. In particular, children's mysterious and spontaneous turning to a religious dimension in life, and their fundamental leaning to love, must be followed, not impeded, by the provision of an atmosphere in which beauty and goodness can flourish.

But what right have teachers of all kinds to communicate knowledge? For Rosmini, there are certain rights which as inborn to human beings cannot be annulled by any society in which persons find themselves. One of these rights is the freedom to develop faculties which lead to human perfection. Amongst these faculties is that of communicating with neighbours for the sake of transmitting (teaching) and receiving (learning) our various experiences. Respecting freedom to teach means not placing obstacles to this faculty whether it is exercised by the learned, the Church, parents or the State. Moreover, this freedom includes the right proper in the educator to decide how the teaching should take place for the benefit of the pupils. But this aspect of Rosmini's pedagogy will be better understood after a discussion of his views on human rights in general.

[39] *Sull'unità dell'educazione*, p. 65.

6. Person and right[40]

In his theory of education Rosmini illustrates principles governing relationships between teacher and pupil. He shows how one person intervenes in the life of another in order to assist with the great work of primary formation (the formation of the person), to which all other kinds of formation are subordinate. In his study of right as the basis of *all* human rights he throws the net wider as he examines the relationships that must exist between human beings as such. These relationships are constituted by duties and rights which must be situated in their source in order to be understood. Only the knowledge of the essence of duty and rights can provide a solid foundation for the philosophy of right and the adequate study of human rights.

Rosmini turns, therefore, to justice as the root and essence of all morality, and expresses its self-evident obligation as follows: 'Acknowledge in practice every being in its order.' A careful analysis of this precept reveals its presuppositions:

1) the activity of an intelligent subject, in so far as the subject is capable of acknowledging in practice what he knows;

2) the activity of a person, that is of the supreme active force within an intelligent subject;

3) good activity, that is, good for the person exercising it;

4) lawful activity, that is, action in harmony with the moral law;

5) activity self-evidently protected by the moral law itself.

These five characteristics constitute the essence of right which Rosmini defines as: 'A faculty to act as one pleases, protected by the moral law which demands respect for this faculty from others.'[41] In other words, the individual's obligation to be just ensures for him the right to act within the limits

---

[40] Cf. *Filosofia del diritto* (Philosophy of Right) [1841-43] *EN*, Padua, 1967-69.

[41] *Ibid.*, vol. 1, part 1, p. 107.

of justice. His duty to act in accordance with justice imposes on others the duty to respect this obligation.

Duty and right are thus co-related in the sense that there can be no right in one person without a corresponding duty in others to respect that right. My duty, for example, to worship God gives rise to my right to worship God, a right which others have a duty to respect. On the other hand, the concept of duty is anterior to that of right and as such does not necessarily give rise to rights in others. For example, my duty to worship God does not necessarily imply that others' rights are violated if I do not worship God as I should.

Individual right

The personal activity constituting the essence of right can be exercised in various ways: a human being can act as an individual or as a member of different societies. These two great divisions of personal activity give rise to two divisions of right made by Rosmini: individual and social right. Each is capable of being exercised when 'a person has dominion over something', because it is his own. This sphere of personal *ownership* (understood not simply in a material sense, but in the broadest meaning of the word, that is, as '*proper* to me, the person') establishes the state of juridical freedom within which the person is free and must be left free. 'What is mine (what I own) constitutes a sphere whose centre is the person. Within this sphere no one can enter.'[42]

But the way in which anything becomes a person's own also provides a foundation for divisions of activity: if what he possesses is his by nature (innate, inborn), his rights are natural, or rational (they are his because he is what he is); if personal ownership is acquired during the course of life, rights are called positive (they are his because of what he does). A complete examination of right would, therefore, have to deal with the following divisions: natural individual right; positive individual right; natural social right; positive social right.

[42] *Ibid.*, vol. 1, p. 160.

The essential, connatural individual right is the human person because person is the 'supreme principle of activity in an intellective being'. In the case of human beings, this supreme activity is brought about by the innate, infinitely dignified light of being which, shining before the human mind, constitutes and establishes it as an active force of intellect and will. It is important to notice that 'person' does not possess right, but — because formed by the light of being — *is* right itself; does not possess freedom, but *is* freedom itself. Every attempt to deprive a person of his supreme activity and thus interrupt the relationship between the human subject and the object which enlightens him intellectually, is an act of violence against the person and consequently an attempt to damage his right as person. All violence against the person as right consists in efforts made to divide the person from truth, virtue and happiness.

The first thing proper to human persons is their nature. Within the sphere constituted by this nature, the person has the right not to be impeded in the decent development of his natural faculties, provided such development does not presume to invade the zone of freedom or juridical dominion proper to others..

The development of natural faculties leads very quickly to the acquisition of natural goods through actions by which persons rightfully take things different from themselves, but not belonging to others, as their own, and use them for their own purposes.

The enjoyment of personal activity and the capacity for ownership, in the sense explained, are rights embodied in the moral law, every infraction of which is itself moral evil. No circumstances can be envisaged relative to what is rightfully owned and to the owning subject which can change such moral evil into good, although there are circumstances, such as lack of use, which dissolve the relationship of ownership and thus leave the field open to other would-be possessors. For Rosmini, therefore, membership of a society, such as the

State, does not and cannot annul these preceding rights even though new relationships do spring from membership of society. The State, for example, cannot absorb the inalienable rights proper to persons, nor can it be considered as more than its individual members in such a way that persons can be sacrificed for the sake of society: 'Let civil society perish ... or be dissolved if this is needed for the salvation of individuals.'[43] Person constitutes the foundation of society, but society is not essential to person.

Social right

Social right arises from the bonds that unite the human being with his neighbour. The bonds themselves are present to form society when a number of people place determined goods in common in order to reach a determined end. Amongst the infinite number of possible societies, three are necessary if human beings are to arrive at perfection on earth and attain their immortal destiny. Rosmini calls them respectively 'theocratic', 'domestic' and 'civil', and restricts his study of social right to them.

Theocratic or *divine society* is that which God wishes to establish with the human race. It is the first society, and as such the basis and foundation of the others. It forms the natural society of the human race, begins with the creation of mankind, and draws its life from the relationships which necessarily unite the creature to God, the supreme Being and absolute Lord of his creatures. Human beings, simply because they are human beings, form a society whose members hold in common truth, virtue and happiness. But God, who is Truth, the Principle of Being, and absolute Good, is the final end of each human being and places in common with his creatures the Good which is himself. The deity acquires a new title of right which he expresses through positive laws, the government of the world, the communication of himself and the sending of ministers who indicate his will.

[43] *Ibid.*, vol. 2, no. 1660.

However, theocratic society arising from creation as such is a rudimentary society. The truth, virtue and happiness that human beings share with God are natural goods, not God himself. Gradually this society is brought to perfection as God reveals himself more and more clearly. Eventually it reaches its perfection in the Incarnation of Jesus Christ, through whom it becomes Church, with its characteristics of unity, holiness and universality. Aggregation to the Church comes about freely through baptism. Constituted through the indwelling of the Holy Spirit, the Church has certain connatural rights — to existence, recognition, free action, and growth — which all must respect. The Church is destined to realise the design of God who wishes all human beings to be united under a single Pastor.

Domestic society is divided into conjugal and parental society. In the former, every good possessed by human beings is put in common, including that of their animal origin. To spiritual goods such as truth, virtue and happiness are added the complementary good that man and woman can offer one another for their mutual enjoyment as a result of their psychological and somatic structure. It is this union of persons of different sex that forms the essence of conjugal society. 'Husband and wife are two human beings who unite in the fullest way possible as man and woman, according to right reason. This is the true concept of marriage.'[44]

Rosmini's view of marriage draws attention to two characteristics. Sexual union, either as a right to be exercised or as actually exercised, constitutes the special aspect of marriage, which must be a full union. In other words, marriage requires and presupposes for the sexual union which marks it out, every other possible union, spiritual and animal, between persons. Moreover, because sexual union demands and perfects every other union between man and woman, it is not and cannot be a merely physical gesture. For Rosmini, sexual union is an act undertaken by the whole human being and

[44] *Ibid.*, vol. 3, no. 997.

constitutes a total, mutual communication at a spiritual level. The outward, physical act is a sign, on the level of sense, of this communion which in its turn entails 1) exclusive love between the spouses, 2) monogamy, 3) the indissolubility of marriage and 4) the need to hold everything in common. In the Church, the marriage bond, already indissoluble by nature, is strengthened by the presence, through grace, of God himself.

With the arrival of children, conjugal society gives rise to parental society in which the parents provide the human nature of their children while the person, the divine image and likeness, is grounded in God himself. As a result, parents' rights extend to the nature of their children, but not to their persons, whose rights are inalienable. And as these persons gradually come to control the exercise of their natural faculties, parental rights begin to decrease and finally cease.

Civil society is for Rosmini the communion desired by several families who wish to entrust the preservation and the regulation of their rights to a single or collective mind called 'government'. This society, therefore, does not have as its end the personal and natural rights of theocratic and conjugal society, but exists simply to oversee the exercise or modality of these rights. Relative to the other two societies, civil society is simply a means to an end; it is not an end in itself.

Two further points about Rosmini's views on civil society must be emphasised even in a brief summary of his work. Both are connected with present-day attitudes to the State. The first reiterates and emphasises what has already been declared about the relationship of civil society to the persons composing it; the second is proper to the government of civil society and raises problems about relating Rosmini's views to the practical requirements of the modern State.

According to Rosmini, the State, despite its universal regulation of the modality of rights, its supremacy over more particular societies, and its stability, has no power to create or destroy human rights. These are already present in the persons composing the State, which exists for the purpose of safeguarding these rights and indeed of enhancing their exercise in so far as this is compatible with the common good (the good of all), the public good (the good of the social body) and private good. Such a position gives the lie to any pretext for totalitarian power on the part of the State.

On the other hand, and this is the second point, Rosmini is decisively opposed to modern notions of democracy. 'One man, one vote' has no place in his view of the establishment of government over the modern State. His practical suggestions in this respect need not delay us here, but the principle on which they are founded is of great interest. For him, a voice in the establishment of government would depend upon the possible contribution made by the members to the well-being of the State. The electoral vote should in some way be proportioned to the interest and responsibility of the citizen in the State. If, for example, we are to accept that there should be no taxation without representation, it would seem logical to require that representation should be in proportion to taxation. The difficulties of such a position were immediately obvious to Rosmini (and are perhaps even more clear to us as taxation, for example, has passed from a merely personal to an impersonal level), but they were not considered as great as the inevitable despotism of the majority which, according to Rosmini, is the ultimate conclusion of 'irresponsible' voting.

Finally, Rosmini's suggestions for the implementation of the art of government are of compelling worth: essential interest, he says, should never be sacrificed to non-essential interests; the totality of utilitarian good, which can never exclude moral good, is to be the ultimate object of government even if this means that sectional interests suffer; expectations should never be greater than the probability of satisfying them; limited well-being, such as economic well-being, should not be given pride of place over total well-being. If this should happen, the inevitable result will be the eventual loss of limited well-being as well as the destruction of civil society as a whole. But it is clear that such suggestions must be considered ultra-utopian as long as there is no system for ensuring that the electoral vote is as far as possible compatible with responsibility for the welfare of the actual State. Voting should never be the expression of a theory or ideology about how the State ought to attain its well-being. Civil society, which bears within itself a natural instinct for improving itself in circumstances as they really are, will never be ruled satisfactorily by the external imposition of any kind of perfectionist theory. In this sense, the pragmatist government that begins from the actual state of society and moves from this point to contributing to the greatest possible genuine satisfaction of its citizens is far more commendable than the facile absolutism associated with ideological government.

7. Person and art[45]

The central position of 'person' in Rosmini's account of anthropological philosophy becomes transparently clear when we encounter his thoughts on the philosophy of art. *Ars artis gratia* would be abhorrent to his vision, in which the perfection of the person, itself dependent upon the light of being, is seen as the source and culmination of all that is worthwhile in human existence. And because his views on art reflect his feelings on every particular aspect of life that seeks complete autonomy and freedom from the restraint of personal integrity, it will be helpful to greater understanding of his general outlook if we consider carefully this aspect of his philosophy.

The artist's tasks, all of which are necessarily imitative in some way, consist in *re*presenting truth and beauty by showing contemporaries how these two things are contained in what they contemplate. The two elements cannot be separated: truth is being as it presents itself to the mind; beauty

---

[45] Cf. *Sull'Idillio e sulla nuova letturatura italiana* (Essay on the Idyll and the New Italian Literature), in *Opuscoli filosofici*, vol. 1, Milan, 1827.

is the order in which being appears, that is, the proportion between the parts of being that we contemplate. In so far as classicism and romanticism try to separate the two, both are inadequate.

Classicism, in taking an 'historical system' as its ideal, is fearful of subordinating truth to beauty; romanticism, which is afraid of sacrificing beauty to truth, tends towards an 'idealist system' in the sense that it wishes to re-present facts as they should be rather than as they are. Neither view takes sufficient account of the presence of sin, or moral evil, in the world: classicism is excessively optimistic and falsifies its re-presentation of reality by excluding all that is evil and hence ugly; romanticism re-presents its own ideals (themselves a limitation of reality), as beautiful, irrespective of any relationship they may have in practice with what actually exists.

The solution, according to Rosmini, is to bring the two sides together through the concept of 'verisimilitude', understood as an attempt to describe something that 'could probably have occurred'. The facts narrated or portrayed need not have happened, but because they *could* have taken place they present some credibility to the artist's contemporaries. In this way, the artist does not risk abandoning the truth — he is not presenting pure invention. At the same time, beauty is not rejected — evil never takes primary place in a work of art.

Rosmini does not neglect the obvious objection to this theory of art. We are not impressing moralism on art, he says: the canons described are merely expressive of reality. The artist does not preach, but he does represent reality as it is. What is ugly is not neglected, but it finds its own level in the great canvas of being where it serves always as a contrast which throws into light the great positive features presented by reality. On the other hand, evil and ugliness are not allowed to assert themselves as though they presented some positive aspect of reality.

It is not difficult to see that behind Rosmini's philosophy of art lies an intense preoccupation with the providence and goodness of the supreme Being whose creation is the object of the artist's contemplation. In the last analysis, art must re-present creation in which 'everything is very good', and towards which even evil must make its contribution.

But Rosmini goes further than offering a basically religious foundation to genuine artistic work. He also maintains that the notion of creation, essentially a Jewish contribution to the understanding of reality but now assimilated by Christianity, provides through revelation an indefinite expansion of the zone of verisimilitude available to the artist. No merely secular imagination, for example, could reach out to depict the Last Supper and the mystery of the Eucharist because these things, and many like them, could never have entered the ambit of secular experience whose limits are essentially restricted to natural and intellectual ideals of beauty. Such imagination cannot reach out to the moral ideal of beauty contained in the totality of things.

Only Christian revelation provides the elements of totality that the human mind looks for in vain with its own powers. Aided by revelation, the artist can seek total truth and beauty, and so come gradually to discover the order and beauty of the universe, furnished as it is with the laws and aims that its Creator has provided for it. It is precisely this possibility of total vision that is always lacking not only in pagan art, but in any branch of knowledge which seeks its own absolute autonomy independently of personal integrity.

Rosmini's philosophy of art was initially developed during the first period of his maturity (1827). Much later in life (1845-55) his understanding of the concept of beauty grew through his examination of the nature of being. His later work[46] posits five elements of beauty: objectivity, unity, plurality, totality, and the mental approval that distinguishes beauty from order. Objectivity enables the artist to seize upon the essence of what he wishes to portray; unity, plurality and

[46] Cf. the chapter *Della bellezza* (On Beauty), in the *Teosofia* (Theosophy) [1859], *EN*, bk 3, Rome, 1938.

totality spring from this essence and permit it to be portrayed in such a way that it elicits applause (the fifth element) from the mind contemplating the universe anew under the direction of the artist.

Although the appreciation of a work of art is not possible for all at the same level — artistic genius and taste, the outcome of natural gifts and education, differ from person to person — everyone is capable of appreciating beauty in some way. Indeed, appreciation on the part of both artist and critic can rise to enthusiasm when the former produces and the latter applauds a work of art that constitutes an imaginative surprise for them both. Such beauty perfects the artist and the beholder, provided it is not isolated from the totality of what is beautiful. In other words, the spirit in contact with beauty becomes itself beautiful if it does not neglect greater for lesser beauty.

The universe itself is a work of art as the execution of a theme present in the mind of the Creator. Human beings, who possess objectivity itself in the idea of being, and thus share in the objective essence and unity of what is created, come through gradual experience (plurality) to appreciate more and more (totality) the beauty of God's work of art as unending 'surprises' are placed before them. God, the supreme Being, who knew from the beginning what he intended in creation, allows us to come little by little to the concrete realisation of that which we know only indeterminately and naturally in the light of being.

8. The Theory of Being[47]

The insistence on 'person' which is such a remarkable feature of Rosmini's philosophy is inevitably reflected in even the briefest summary of his work. Unfortunately such insistence often serves to distract attention from the difficult but

[47] Cf. *Teosofia*, *EN*, vol 4, *Del divino nella natura* (The divine in nature).

intensely rewarding task awaiting those who wish to follow Rosmini on the final stage of his philosophical journey.

For ten years before his death he laboured, as time and other work permitted, on a description of all that can be known about being itself. He passed from studying the person who knows to the study of what is known.

In part, this is the logical consequence of his philosophy of person. As we have seen, free, personal dignity depends ultimately upon our acknowledgement of what we know. Consequently, this dignity will depend upon the dignity of what is known, of what is acknowledged. There can be no final treatise of 'person' until at least some consideration has been given to the object of the essential knowledge possessed by persons.

This inevitably draws Rosmini's studies into the sphere of being as such. But once this field has been entered, attention is focused upon the whole range of what is. 'Person' takes its place as part of being, and begins to be seen within the totality of being. Nothing of person is lost when it takes its place in being, although being becomes inevitably the centre of interest.

In fact, the objects known by the human mind fall under one of three headings: the idea, which is the centre and foundation of all knowledge; the intelligent soul or human subject, which is the centre and foundation of all knowing activity; and being, the centre and foundation of all that is contained in thought. The idea and the human soul are studied in the theory of knowledge and in philosophical psychology, which Rosmini had already undertaken and brought to a conclusion; being would be the object of his last work under the general title *Theosophy*, that is, 'wisdom in relationship to God' (the meaning of 'theosophy' accepted by Rosmini — it is not to be understood in its modern significance of 'eclectic teaching about God').

Being however, can be regarded in three ways. Considered as the object of intuition, that is, in its essence, it is the object of ontology; considered in its adequate term, that is, in God, it becomes the object of natural theology; and considered in its inadequate terms, that is, in terms which do not exhaust its potential, it is the object of cosmology.

Ontology

The aim of ontology is to research the nature and essential characteristics of being. This in turn leads to the central and constantly recurring problem about being: how can its unity be reconciled with its multiplicity? If being must essentially be one, as is indeed the case, how can we be involved, as indeed we are, with a multiplicity of beings?

Rosmini looks to the concept of 'virtual being' for an answer to the problem. Indetermination, as we have seen in the theory of knowledge, is an essential characteristic of being. Being can take on any kind of determination. This potentiality of being is the foundation upon which things depend for their unity in being and their multiplicity amongst themselves.

To think of being as potential or virtual means considering it as one and multiple. Multiplicity, however, is not only thinkable; it exists as a fact intrinsic to being and is present in being through the *modes* of being, the first classification of all possible entities. In other words, being, while remaining one and integral, possesses contemporaneously three essential modes, ideal, real and moral, all of which are unfolded in the non-essential manifestations of being. These modes reside in the very constitution of being as the roots in which all non-essential modes of being are founded.

The ideal mode of being is the pure knowableness proper to intelligible being; real being is the concrete, substantial subsistence of individuals; moral being expresses the harmony or synthesis of the other two modes.

The three modes are therefore co-present in being. At the same time, each of them *necessarily* requires the others. Intelligible or ideal being is understandable of its nature, but could not be so without the presence of some real being capable of understanding it; simultaneously, this real being, which is made up of feeling and intelligence, implies the existence of an intelligent subject, a moral being, who unites the essence of being (the ideal mode) with feeling (the real mode). This, according to Rosmini, is the 'law of the synthesis of being' and it is expressed as follows: 'Being cannot exist under one of the three forms unless it also exists under the other two.' Another law, consequent on the 'synthesis' of being, is that of the reciprocal in-existence or 'circuminsession' of the three forms: every form of being is all being, although in its own way. Each form, considered as the whole of being, must therefore contain in itself the other two modes, even if it contains them in its own mode of being.

Natural theology

God is the infinite, real Being. But according to Rosmini, what is real can be perceived only by means of feeling. Human beings possess feeling, but only a finite feeling which cannot therefore be the vehicle of the perception of an infinite reality such as God. Nevertheless, by means of ideal being, we can come to understand the necessity of God's existence while remaining ignorant of how he exists and what he is. Ideal being, with its characteristics of eternity, necessity and immateriality, is something divine, and as such provides us with a sufficient notion of the God whose existence we cannot but affirm. At the same time, the possibility proper to this mode of being prevents any confusion between it and the living, actual, operating reality which is God. This distinction between the possibility of being and its actuality requires that the idea of being, the means by which we acknowledge the existence of God, remain unconfused with God himself.

But the divine characteristics of the idea of being, 'this kind of divine ray which penetrates created nature', do explain the likeness or common element present between the form of finite beings and God. It is in virtue of this likeness that communication is possible between beings and God; it explains how the leap from what is created to the existence of God can be made by analogy or proportion. According to Rosmini, who does not exclude *a posteriori* proofs of the existence of God, this *a priori* method is the better way of proving God's existence. It requires that we set off from the idea of being, and arrive at the necessity of the existence of God.

For example, if truth or intelligible being exists, an infinite mind, capable of producing this idea, must exist. Such an infinite mind cannot not be God. Again, virtual or possible being is inexhaustible in its finite realisations. This would be impossible if it were not related to an adequate real, infinite term (the relationship with the finite human mind is not sufficient to explain it), which must therefore exist. Again, the possibility upon which the existence of every real being depends (unless a thing is possible, it cannot exist in any way) is present only in a mind. Things are possible only to the extent that they are conceived mentally. The human mind, however, cannot know in their possibility all the real things that exist; they must therefore be known by a superior mind (God) who knows all things.

In all these proofs there is a common mode of procedure. The existence of God is necessary for the existence of intelligible being; but intelligible being certainly exists; therefore the existence of God is necessary.

Having demonstrated the existence of God, Rosmini endeavours to see what light can be thrown by reason on the revealed mystery of God as one in nature and triune in persons. He does not intend to demonstrate the mystery, but indicate its fittingness which follows from the teaching on the three forms of being and their reciprocal circuminsession. He concludes that these 'natural' modes of being are not persons, and hence do not constitute the Trinity, but that the relationships between them help us to form an admittedly imperfect image of the three divine Persons.

Creation, the *ad extra* activity of the Almighty by means of which the universe comes into existence, is another field of natural theology considered by Rosmini. Here, too, his intention is not to prove the doctrine, but through reason to show its fittingness and penetrate it more deeply.

Ideal being shows the possibility of the existence of real beings. The actual existence of beings that need not have existed shows in its turn that creation has been necessary for their subsistence — without creation they would not have existed. Moreover, by remaining in existence, they experience a continual creation through their conservation.

Creation comes about through the *ad extra* act of God which, although unknown in itself to the human mind, can be glimpsed through analogy. It occurs, says Rosmini, in three stages (he is speaking of our way of considering it, of course: — in God the act of creation is as simple as God himself).

First, theosophical abstraction, as he calls it, distinguishes in the Word of God the beginning and the term of knowledge, that is, being and reality. Being, divided from its term but now considered as capable of actualisation in various real ways, is called 'initial being'. This being, abstracted from the Word and revealed to us in the light of reason, is not God, but the 'divine' of which we have spoken.

Second, after the abstraction of initial being, God considers all the finite real things that could constitute the terms of this being. In doing so he 'imagines' the reality of the universe which as limited being is lovable, and hence loved by God, who loves everything that can be an object of love.

Third, God produces the divine synthesis in which he unites initial being with the limited realities he 'imagines'. This union brings about the actual, rather than the 'imagined' creation of finite beings. All these beings can in their turn reach out to him by means of the humans in their midst who, as the apex of creation, can in some way know God, communicate with him, enjoy him and unite themselves with him. All other beings on earth are subordinate to human beings, whose nature is destined, through grace, to be deified, that is, to share in the divinity itself on a supernatural level.

The final end of creation, therefore, is a dialogue between the human, intelligent creature and God, whose works human beings acknowledge by praising the holiness, power, wisdom and love of the Creator. God provides the stimulus for this by governing the world with laws which manifest his intelligence, power and goodness, and ensure the greatest possible good at the cost of the least possible evil.

Cosmology[48]

The object of cosmology is real, finite being which according to Rosmini obeys what he calls the 'law of synthesism'. This law requires that all the parts of real, finite being have a necessary, twofold bond which unites them amongst themselves and with God, the absolute Being. Every time that a finite being is considered as though it were altogether separate from the other parts of creation and from God, error and absurdity result.

The fundamental problem of cosmology is to determine exactly the nature of reality. For Rosmini, this is constituted by feeling, which in its turn leads us to that first act or intimate essence of what is real, by which we know things in our perception of them. This 'stuff of being', as he calls it, is the essential element of the pure, simple reality of finite being, and it is the means of communication between one real thing and another.

Real, finite things do not possess the totality of being and are therefore relative or incomplete. But intelligent beings can be said to be relatively complete by means of being which they possess in its ideal form. They are different from God who is absolutely complete, but they share nevertheless in what is proper to him alone. And as such they constitute his image and likeness here on earth.

[48] Only fragments remain of Rosmini's notes on this subject. Cf. *Teosofia, EN*, vol. 8.

Chapter 3.

Rosmini's Theological Teaching[49]

Introduction

DESPITE the systematic attention paid at least in Italy to his philosophical teaching, Rosmini's theology and the theological aspects of his philosophical output have been largely ignored. There are many reasons for this, amongst them the originality of certain treatises and hypotheses of his which gave rise to bitter polemics; the lack of any organic treatment of theology, caused by Rosmini's other occupations which prevented him from completing his theological works; the suspicion of heterodoxy after the condemnation by the Church of forty propositions, mostly theological in character, taken posthumously from Rosmini's works; and the need for familiarity with Rosmini's fundamental philosophical principles prior to the study of his theology.

Nevertheless, theology was of extreme importance to Rosmini himself who considered it both as the point of arrival of philosophy, and as a kind of 'golden cupola' resting on the edifice of philosophy and human knowledge, which it protects and embellishes. Theology even plays its part in human knowledge by raising questions which would otherwise be

---

[49] Cf. *Antropologia soprannaturale* (Supernatural Anthropology) [1884], *EN*, Roma, 1955; *L'introduzione del vangelo secondo Giovanni commentata* (Commentary on the Introduction to the Gospel according to John) [1882], *EN*, Padua, 1966; *Il razionalismo che tenta insinuarsi nelle scuole teologiche* (Rationalism and its Attempt to Infiltrate the Theological Schools) [1882], *EN*, Padua. 1967; *Dell'idea della sapienza* (The Idea of Wisdom), in the *Introduzione alla filosofia* [1850], *EN*, Rome, 1934.

totally neglected by philosophy — the nature of 'body', for example, is inevitably re-examined in the light of the mystery of the Eucharist.

In Rosmini's 'system of truth', theology is considered from two points of view. Although its object is always the supreme Being, God, theology may be confined within the limits of unaided natural reason (natural theology), or treat of God as he is known through the data provided by revelation only (positive theology). Data which can be known by reason, whether it is in fact known by reason or with the help of revelation, is the object of natural theology.

In natural and positive theology we are dealing with *branches of knowledge*, and it is this characteristic which distinguishes theology of any kind from religion. 'Theology is a science; religion is action; the former is knowledge, or theory, the latter worship, or practice ... the theologian is not always a religious person, and the religious person is not always a theologian.'[50] Religion is present when spiritual beliefs issue in interior and exterior actions of adoration and prayer. Religion becomes supernatural when God himself acts in the human spirit with what Christians call 'grace'.

Grace

We have already spoken about Rosmini's natural theology under the heading 'The Theory of Being', when we saw that little can be known about God with the light of reason alone. We can affirm his existence, and certain characteristics of his essence such as his goodness, justice and perfection, but we cannot know them positively or directly because we lack experience of God. Naturally speaking, we do not know him concretely and really in the way that we know the created things which fall under our sense-experience. Hence the theologian who speaks of God on the basis of natural reason alone is like a person blind from birth who speaks of sight: different arguments allow him to affirm the existence of sight,

[50] *AS, EN*, vol 1, p. 27.

but without his grasping positively the reality of what he can affirm.

Such affirmation requires the real perception of the object of affirmation. In our case, God must be perceived really. But this can only happen if God offers himself to be perceived; God acts in the human spirit without any possibility that human beings can bring this about as, for instance, they could produce new feelings through their natural activity. Such an action freely given on God's part is what we call 'grace'. It constitutes the essence of supernatural religion and the object of positive theology.

Grace, therefore, is a real, efficacious action, a force, 'an interior, powerful aid'. It operates in the intellective essence of the human soul because 'the supreme Being can communicate only with what is most noble in the human being.'[51] In the essence of the human spirit the real, immanent action of God produces a supernatural feeling which although passively received, as every feeling is, produces in human beings an action corresponding to the nature itself of the feeling. In other words, 'a truly new principle of action', called by Rosmini an 'instinct of the Holy Spirit', arises in the essence of the soul and allows us to speak of 'a new creature', who as 'reborn' is capable of entering the kingdom of heaven.[52]

Deiform grace

Not all God's actions are equal. For example, creation and the government of the world begin in God, but terminate in something produced by God's operation, that is, in something altogether different from God. Such operations are divine. Grace, however, is a 'deiform' operation, in which God is principle (beginning) and term (end) of the action. Through the action of grace, God is formally united to the human being and constitutes for the human spirit raised up to the supernatural level what we may call its 'quasi-form'.

[51] *Ibid.*, p. 48.
[52] Cf. *ibid.*, p. 59.

In positing God as the form of the understanding, Rosmini would seem to run the risk of falling into pantheism. But God, Rosmini would reply, is the *objective* form of the human spirit, and as such is present to the spirit without becoming part of it (just as light allows us to see without its becoming part of ourselves). At the same time, he is not present to the spirit in the way that, on a natural level, ideal being is present to the intellectual soul as its natural form. Ideal being allows us to intuit being in its initial mode; but through grace we perceive Being in its term so that the substance of Being becomes the form of our supernatural reality.

As we have seen, God's operation creates a supernatural feeling in the human spirit. We feel God operating in us and simultaneously we experience the presence of a feeling of perfect satisfaction. This feeling does not, however, necessarily bring consciousness in its wake. In fact, grace as creative (in its first act on the spirit) cannot be adverted to, just as our natural creation cannot be adverted to. Other acts of grace, which can be adverted to, are known only with difficulty. But the *effects* of grace, 'love, joy, peace, patience, kindness, goodness, faithfulness, gentleness, self-control' (Gal 5.22-23), are easily recognised.

Moreover, grace is not the final action of God in the human spirit. The supreme Being reveals himself through grace indistinctly, not clearly. The certainty of the interior presence of the ALL is not accompanied by a perception which is total: *totum, sed non totaliter*, as the theologians say. Faith begins with the indistinct perception of God, and draws us on to what remains hidden of God.

> This hidden part of God, this mysterious presence, is properly speaking the object of faith and the vehicle of grace. It is the divine stimulus, the goad, as it were, of the divine substance with which God touches the human being.[53]

When God is perceived distinctly, as he is in the other life, we pass from a state of grace to a state of glory.

[53] *Ibid.*, p. 65.

Triniform grace

The grace which unites human beings to God is the indwelling of the divine substance in the soul. United to God in this way, we enter into the life of the one God in three Persons, Father, Son and Holy Spirit. Thus Rosmini lays the foundation for his understanding of the distinction between deiform and triniform grace.

The feeling imparted by deiform grace is of some indistinct ALL which encloses within itself every possible force and energy. But the same feeling imparted by triniform grace is of an ALL unfolded to the human spirit in three modes. The same ALL is now perceived as a creative force, the source of every other force, and gives rise to the 'fear of the Lord'; it is perceived as knowledge of God which enlightens the intellect and gives rise to faith; it is perceived as willed love of God and gives rise to perfect satisfaction. The feeling of omnipotent force that acts, of subsistent truth that illumines, and of unlimited love that expands and attracts the will, comprises triniform grace.

Although deiform and triniform grace do not differ in essence, they possess different grades in the sense that the first can be perceived by human beings without the second. There will be times when God gives to human beings the capacity to perceive the one but not the other. Thus for Rosmini, the grace of the Old Testament is pre-eminently deiform; of the New Testament, pre-eminently triniform.

When the human spirit is in possession of triniform grace, or rather possessed by it, humans come to the final perfection for which their nature and the gift of God has made them suitable. On the level of nature, in contradistinction to the supernatural level, we find ourselves open to the infinity of ideal being but at the same time in possession of only limited satisfaction through feeling that can never actually exhaust the infinite *possibilities* revealed to us in the idea. This natural imbalance drives us to seek something really infinite, or infinite knowledge, or infinite love, any one of which will envelop the others and bring us to the infinite Being who alone can put an end to human travail. The search, however, is destined to failure. We cannot satisfy these exigencies of ours. But God, in revealing the mystery of the blessed Trinity, furnishes us with the final link of the chain. Triniform grace, which will one day be triniform glory, constitutes life, knowledge and love operating supernaturally within the human being. Truth and love find their definitive meeting place in God: 'the work of Christian *wisdom* truly consists in this *charity* exercised in *truth*.'[54] Religion, and philosophy also, find their completion in Christian wisdom where 'charity is simply the execution and the substantiation of truth.'[55]

Original sin

Within the context of the divine economy, grace is imparted through Christ. The revealed religion which he has brought us is based essentially on two truths: original sin and redemption. Grace comes to us therefore in the circumstances provided by original sin and our redemption.

The first human beings committed sin, and committed it freely, losing grace and the fruits of the grace which they had possessed from the beginning. Their human will remained, but without the capacity to command the other human faculties. Indeed, disordered in itself, it produced disorder in the faculties dependent upon it and, as the supreme activity within human beings, provided the basis for that twist of human nature called in them and their descendants 'original sin'. But the difference between original sin in our first parents and in us lies in the quality of will with which the one, same sin is incurred. In Adam and Eve, the will is free and therefore guilty of fault as well as of sin. In us, original sin, although an act of the will, is not free. Deprived of grace through Adam's sin, his descendants have no choice at the moment of conception. They have no means of withdrawing their will from

[54] *Ibid.*, p. 152.
[55] *Ibid.*, p. 174.

submission to their human instincts and turning it to God as their supreme Good. The supreme activity of the will, dedicated now to what is less than God, has turned, but not freely, from the supreme Good to a lesser good, and surrendered to it entirely. According to Rosmini, disordered nature necessarily infects the person of the newly conceived human being.

Rosmini's distinction between sin and fault, which he used to safeguard the true nature of sin in the newly conceived, was intended as a defence against the errors of Baius, who maintained that the human will was irredeemably corrupt and impervious to the healing power of interior grace, and the opposite errors of Pelagius and the Jansenists who thought that only some exterior help was needed for us to act supernaturally. Rosmini was to come under severe attack for his teaching on original sin, and in particular for his distinction between sin and fault.

Redemption

Within the circumstances created by sin in the human race, God helped human beings by means of revelation and grace. The principle of supernatural revelation, and therefore of grace, is Christ, known incipiently in the Old Testament through the gradual unveiling of the divine plan of redemption, and known fully in the New Testament through the Incarnation.

It is the humanity of Christ that provides the vehicle for the manifestation of the Word of God who, through his body, communicates with his fellows and provides them with the necessary sanctifying grace, obtained through his death and resurrection, to raise them from sin. Having gone up to his Father, he now unites himself with his brethren on earth through the sacraments. These are signs which effectively bring us into contact, in various ways, with the human nature of Christ, and hence with his divine healing power. In other words, the grace that now saves mankind is a communication of the Word to human beings through the human nature assumed by the Word. According to Rosmini, this explains why we speak of 'incorporation in Christ,' and of incorporation in him as the beginning of eternal life.

> The solemn phrase 'in Christ' contains a summary of the whole of Christianity because it expresses the real mystical union of human beings with Christ. This union and incorporation constitutes Christianity in act,[56]

the visible effect of which in this world is the establishment of the Church of Jesus Christ.

Character

According to Rosmini, union and incorporation with Christ is made up of two elements. The first establishes a stable contact between Christ and the human spirit, and is brought about by the work of Christ at the moment of baptism when the light of the Word is impressed upon the soul, leaving there an indelible mark or character which distinguishes Christians from non-Christians. Such 'enlightenment' provides the soul with new, supernatural capacities enabling it to receive and administer the sacraments, and placing it once and for all on a supernatural level. The character is also the fount of grace within the Christian.

When the character is left to expand its power unhindered in the Christian, grace, the second element of incorporation in Christ, enters and informs the will of the Christian (only sin, by which the will impedes the action of the character, prevents final incorporation in Christ).

Thus it is Christ himself, 'the human, perfect nature of Christ, triumphant over death',[57] who operates in and with the Christian. One of Rosmini's own prayers is in line with this truth. 'Father,' he prays, 'as your divine Son would pray in me, so I would pray to you.'[58] Moreover, as a result of the interior union between Christ and his disciple, two basic feelings are present in the Christian: that by which he perceives his own

[56] *IG*, p. 153.

[57] *Ibid*.

[58] *Rosminian Spirituality*, p. 405.

nothingness, and that which speaks to him of his dignity, power and greatness. The former is the source of the Christian's humility; the latter provides that greatness of soul which enables the Christian to undertake anything whatsoever in the service of his Lord, and consider all things as loss for the sake of serving him.

Christian life in the Church

It is clear that for Rosmini, Christian living is reduced ultimately to the Christian's grace-inspired willingness to allow the Spirit of Christ himself to have the final word in all that the human person thinks and does. Rosmini prays:

> O God, may your Spirit be the spring of all my activity and all my acts. Let everything in me come from you, nothing from myself.[59]

The spiritual endeavour of the Christian is nothing more than the effort and sacrifice he makes to die to self and live according to the Spirit of Christ within him. The struggle which looms so large in every truly Christian existence is again the outcome of the presence within the soul of two elements: the wounded, disordered nature of the human being, and the life of Christ himself. The decision facing the Christian consists in the choice he has to make of living in accord with one or other of these elements. If he chooses life in the Pauline sense, the outcome will be expressed in the words: 'I live, yet not I. It is Christ who lives in me' (Gal 2.20).

The life of Christ will therefore draw the Christian to love and desire the things that Christ desired, and supremely to devote his life in whatever way he can to the well-being of the Church founded by Christ which, as the 'supernatural society of mankind', is the beginning on earth of the kingdom, the final source of the glory of God and the good of humanity. In the Church, the Christian will find the strength he needs, above all through the sacraments of confirmation and the Eucharist, to seek 'first, the kingdom of God and his justice'

[59] *Ibid.*, p. 409.

(Mt 6.33), the will of God as the source of all his thoughts and actions, and the humble, untiring service of his neighbour.

Baptism, Confirmation, the Eucharist

Rosmini's writings on baptism, confirmation and the Eucharist offer special insight into the nature and effects of these three sacraments of initiation which sanctify the whole human being, mind, will and body.

As we have seen, baptism impresses the light of the Word on the human spirit. Through this light, the Word continually offers the spirit an object of love that can draw the soul's will away from its mortal preoccupation with self, and thus release it from the sin in which it was conceived. Moreover baptism, according to Rosmini, brings to the soul the *gifts* of the Spirit in the wake of the Christ-life.

Confirmation, which confers the presence of the *person* of the Holy Spirit on the Christian soul, impresses the character more deeply in the human spirit, 'confirming' all that has already been gifted, assuring Christians of the indwelling of the third Person of the blessed Trinity in their souls, and baptising them with fire intended to set the whole world ablaze.

But the crown of the sacramental system is the Eucharist, 'the most ineffable of all the sacraments,'[60] as Rosmini calls it. According to the hypothesis advanced by Rosmini, transubstantiation, or the conversion of the whole substance of the bread and wine into the substance of the body and blood of Christ, 'takes place in a way analogous to that in which we convert the food we eat, through nutrition, into our own body and blood.'[61] The change takes place by means of a supernatural operation,[62] with which the Word appropriates the substance of the bread and wine, making it the substance of his own body. When we eat the body of Christ and drink his

[60] *AS, EN*, vol 2, p. 275.

[61] *Ibid.*, p. 276.

[62] *Ibid.*, p. 297.

blood, however, it is we who are assimilated into Christ through the superior power of his divine humanity which allows us to share in his eternal life. Indeed, the body of Christ of which we have partaken assures us of life after death when, until the resurrection of the body, we shall be without any corporeal element other than that granted to us through our assimilation into the life of Christ.

Baptism, confirmation and the Eucharist together re-create the whole human being. Although each of these sacraments brings in its wake at least indirectly the effects of them all, it is in baptism principally that the Christian's intellect is enlightened anew by the light of the Word; in confirmation that the Christian's will is renewed by person of the Holy Spirit, Love in person; and in the Eucharist that his body receives the seed of Christ's resurrected life which ensures the Christian a share in the resurrection itself.

Chapter 4.

Controversies

AS WE HAVE SEEN, Rosmini's life was punctuated by attacks on his philosophical and theological works. Some of these attacks, and Rosmini's own defence against them, were made in language that today would be considered intemperate. Some were motivated by antipathy to new ideas, or by the conservative attitude then thought by many to be a necessary bulwark against revolutionary idealism inside and outside the Church.

Politics also played a part in the problems which beset Rosmini almost as soon as he came to maturity. As a defender of church freedom, he was the object of suspicion from every totalitarian regime with which he was in contact; as an ardent believer in the impossibility of restraining nationalistic fervour in Italy, many of his ideas were not acceptable to the authorities of the Austrian Empire, of which he was a subject, nor to the feeling prevalent in ecclesiastical diplomacy at a time when the temporal authority of the papacy needed to be secured, it was thought, against every possible inroad. Nor did Rosmini's position as founder of a religious congregation save him from what could be construed as opposition springing from misunderstanding of his calling, and misapprehension of new applications of principle in the religious life.

But such opposition would have been seen for what it was — the rough and tumble of history refining the comprehension of Rosmini's teaching and activity — if two facts had not intervened to produce almost total obliteration of Rosmini's contribution to philosophy and theology. The first occurred during his lifetime, the second posthumously.

1848, the 'year of revolutions', saw the flight of Pope Pius IX from Rome to Gaeta. The crisis, precipitated by the assassination of Pellegrino Rossi, the papal Prime Minister, on November 15th, brought about a change of policy in Roman diplomacy which from now on stood out against the cause of Italian unity. Rosmini, who saw that the unity of the Italian nation was inevitable, hoped for the founding of a confederation of Italian states, the only way, as he saw it, of safeguarding the independence of the Papacy.

> It is foolish to think that anything can deter a nation from attaining its unanimous desire. It is even more foolish to imagine that its desire can be deterred by insignificant forces. The nation will overcome all obstacles; its impetus can be illuminated and controlled, but never impeded. It is extremely probable therefore that the present movement in Italy will not end until the country has become a nation ... There seems no way of avoiding [the dangers facing the Church] unless the desired unity of Italy is promoted by means of a Confederation of Italian states.[63]

It was to further this purpose that Rosmini found himself in Rome during the fatal last days of Rossi. Having accepted the office of special legate of the Piedmontese government, which he repudiated when his own conditions for mediation between the Pope and the Piedmontese were abandoned, he followed Pius IX, at the Pope's request, to Gaeta. His presence at the Papal court and the favour he enjoyed from the Pope, were an obvious embarrassment to the pro-Austrian policy of Cardinal Antonelli, and it was not long before the pressure put on Pius IX to abandon his constitutional views was reflected in Rosmini's request to leave Gaeta for Naples, where he spent a great part of his time (from 24th January 1849) writing his unfinished *Introduzione del vangelo secondo Giovanni commentata* (Commentary on the Introduction to the Gospel according to John), a sublime mystical and metaphysical work.

Rosmini saw the Pope again at Gaeta some months later, on

---

[63] To Cardinal Castracane, 25th May 1848, *EC*, vol. 3, p. 323.

June 9th, 1849, three days after Pius IX had confirmed a decree of the Congregation of the Index placing Rosmini's *Cinque piaghe della santa Chiesa* and his *Costituzione civile secondo la giustizia sociale* amongst the list of prohibited books. Of this decree Rosmini knew nothing, nor did the Pope mention it either then or during the last audience Rosmini had with him on June 14th. Only on August 15th, on his return journey to Stresa, was Rosmini informed at Albano near Rome of the decree, to which he submitted humbly and completely. This prohibition was the first incident which set Rosmini apart from the great following which had been his until that moment.

The tragedy of the prohibition lay, however, not only in the discrediting of Rosmini in ecclesiastical eyes, but also in the extinction of the one spiral of light which might have prevented the Church's closing in on herself in so many ways for the next century. And Rosmini's prophecy about the total loss of the Papal states was in fact fulfilled:

> If a monarchy or a republic were to come to power as a single State in Italy ... the States of the Church would inevitably be lost. Even Rome would go the same way, because that city alone would be suitable as a capital.[64]

Moreover, Rosmini's appeal in the *Five Wounds of the Church* for renewal of liturgical life in the Church, for reform of education amongst the clergy, for unity among the bishops, for consultation with the people, for freedom from governmental pressure in the choice of new bishops, and for proper use of the Church's temporalities, was to remain practically unheeded until the second Vatican Council. Only after the end of the Council, and some two months before the abolition of the *Index* itself in July 1966, was licence given by the Cardinal Ottaviani, Pro-Prefect of the Congregation for the Doctrine of the Faith (which succeeded to the work of the Congregation of the Index, and the Holy Office) for the book to be printed once more.[65]

[64] *Ibid.*

The prohibition of these two works did not put an end to the attacks on Rosmini's position during the remainder of his life or after his death. However, the decree *Dimittantur* of 1854, in which all his published works were declared free of heterodoxy, did ensure that the debate continued on more or less acceptable lines for about twenty years. Certainly, it lacked the venom which had earlier characterised it.

After Rosmini's death, and despite the *Dimittantur*, hostilities were renewed with great vigour in the second half of the 1870's as Leo XIII continued the work of rehabilitation of Thomism, a process which culminated in 1879 with the publication of the encyclical *Aeterni Patris*. Revived interest in St. Thomas, which Rosmini himself had encouraged in all his writings, led to the adoption by churchmen of Neo-Thomism as their quasi-official philosophy, and to an attempt to outlaw every other kind of rational thought within ecclesiastical circles. In particular, any philosophy which projected notions of an intuitive, natural bond of truth between the Creator and human beings was looked upon with great suspicion. In other words, a philosophy which would depend for its first principles upon a natural light of truth was not acceptable.

The position of Neo-Thomism within church circles took on the appearance of what we may call 'dogmatic' philosophy, a branch as it were of the field of dogma in which the Church as Church possessed its own authority. Only 'dogmatic' philosophy would answer the need keenly felt by many ecclesiastics to defend the political 'rights' of the Church. Despite the genuine effort of Leo XIII to come to terms with the ills of modern, capitalist society,[66] the still lingering conception of the Church as a hegemony in a worldly sense required the 'appropriation' of a philosophy which would be able to sustain ecclesiastico-political requirements. The limitations of such a stance were soon to be revealed in the upsurge of

[65] Cf. S. Congregazione per la dottrina della fede, prot. n. 9/66 (unedited), 27th April 1966.

[66] Cf. the encyclical, *Rerum novarum*, 1891.

Modernism, against which dogmatism, in the philosophical sense, was powerless.

In the meantime, 40 propositions taken from posthumous and non-posthumous works of Rosmini had been condemned in the decree *Post Obitum*.[67] Under suspicion as teachings which *catholicae veritati haud consonae videbantur* (seemed scarcely to accord with catholic truth), these propositions were condemned as *reprobandae*, *damnandae*, and *proscribendae* (to be reproved, condemned and proscribed) without, however, falling under any theological note. In other words, they were not condemned as 'heretical', 'offensive to pious ears', or damnable in any specific way, and no attempt was made in the document to connect their condemnation with the suspicion which had caused their delation.

Three things stand out concerning this condemnation. First, the delation of the propositions as *catholicae veritati haud consonae* indicates that the difficulties raised by the teaching underlying the propositions were felt to be theological, rather than philosophical. No other meaning can be given to the phrase 'catholic truth'. Second, the first 24 propositions are nevertheless concerned with philosophical matters, and in particular with the question of the intellectual relationship between the creature and the Creator. It was obviously felt as essential that Rosmini's view of such a relationship should be undermined from the beginning. Third, the immense difficulties under which the compilers laboured to produce the propositions is clear from the way in which several of the propositions are stitched together. The most obvious example is found in no. 12: *Finita realitas non est, sed Deus facit eam addendo infinitae realitati limitationem. Esse initiale fit essentia omnis entis realis. Esse quod actuat naturas finitas ipsis coniunctum, est recisum a Deo* (Finite reality is not, but God makes it be by adding limitation to infinite reality. Initial being becomes the essence of every real being. Being, which

---

[67] 14th December, 1887; published 7th March, 1888.

actuates finite natures, having been joined to them, is cut off from God).

This proposition, although taken from the *Teosofia*, a single, posthumous work, and made to run as a single assertion, is composed of sentences scattered across many pages and taken from more than one volume of the book, as the following translation of Rosmini's own words, and references to their sources, makes clear:

'Finite reality is not, but he [God] makes it be by adding limitation to infinite reality' (*Teosofia*, vol 1, n. 681).

'Initial being ... becomes the *essence* of every real being' (*Ibid.*, n. 458).

'Being, which actuates finite natures, joined with these by being cut off from God ...' (vol. 3, n. 1425).

The practical impossibility of giving any meaning to these words without reference to their context is itself indicative of the difficulties faced by the compilers who intended to offer Proposition 12 as evidence of pantheism in Rosmini. His genuine views on this matter are, however, clearly expressed in the following passage from his *Commentary on the Introduction to the Gospel according to John*:

> When there is question of the modes in which the divine subsistence is limited, we do not mean that the divine substance receives, or can receive limitations. However, the divine substance is *being*, and consequently being which, as its concept shows, is able to be in two modes, unlimited and limited. Unlimited and unchangeable being is proper to the divine substance; limited being is proper to the creature. The divine substance contains therefore the *possibility* of creatures because in it is to be found being which *can* be limited. But the creature is not present in the divine substance. What is present — because being is present, and being contains in its concept the *possibility* of limitation — is the reason underlying the creature's possibility of existence.
>
> The *possibility* proper to creatures is, however, twofold: *logical* and *physical*. The logical possibility is the idea, or the reason underlying creaturehood; the physical possibility is the power, or efficient cause of the creature, that is, the

creative power. Absolute being, therefore, contains in its concept both the idea of limited being, that is, of the creature, and the power to produce the creature, that is, to render real and subsisting the limited being manifest in the idea. In a word, the absolute being possesses all that is needed to make itself creator, creator of limited being, of the creature, by making the creature real and subsistent'[68]

It is matters of this kind which have prompted the re-examination of the 40 propositions by a commission of the Congregation for the Doctrine of the Faith which began its work in the autumn of last year (1991). But there is no doubt that for almost the whole of this century the propositions attained the end for which they were intended: Rosmini's work stood no chance of acceptance, or even impartial examination, by the mainstream of Catholic thought. And lacking a home base, as it were, it has inevitably been unable to penetrate the world at large. Now that attitudes have changed, mainly through the devoted work of the few who stood by his 'system of truth' during the period of persecution, it is to be hoped that his work will have the general acceptance it deserves.

[68] *EN*, p.27-28.

Chapter 5.

The Interior Life

'ADVERSITY does not weaken a person; it shows him for what he is.' This formidable statement, suitably adapted from a striking phrase in the *Imitation of Christ*, makes it clear that we can use the controversies which plagued the last years of Rosmini's life as privileged vantage points from which to view his inner spirit.

There are, of course, other ways of approaching the subject. Rosmini wrote a great number of spiritual books which express not only his teaching but the feelings of his heart;[69] his vast correspondence provides us with a clear outline of the advice he gave others about the inner life;[70] his published sermons[71] offer a mine of information about the ascetical life and the faith-principles underlying it. But the immense extent of the available matter, spread over subjects as diverse as the heights of mystical prayer and the need to ensure the physical well-being of the missioners whom he sent to work in Great Britain and Ireland, is of secondary importance in illustrating the well-springs of Rosmini's own deepest thoughts and actions. Compared with his counsel to others, and his theological teaching, his own reaction to spiritual pain and dereliction must provide the basic material for our fundamental understanding of his spiritual teaching and of the kind of person he really was.

[69] E.g. *Manuale del esercitatore* (Manual for the retreat giver) [1840], CrE. 1987.

[70] *Epistolario Ascetico*, Rome, 1911.

[71] *Prose Ecclesistiche* [1840], *La Dottrina della Carità*, CrE., Stresa, 1985; *Discorsi parrocchiali*, CrE., Stresa, 1986.

The nature of that reaction is shown best of all at the moment of the ecclesiastical prohibition of the *Cinque piaghe della santa chiesa* and the *Costituzione secondo la giustizia sociale*. From then on, Rosmini stood condemned in the eyes of many of his contemporaries as an acknowledged danger to the Church, to which he had devoted his life and work. But to understand that reaction at its deepest level, we need to recall how he had undertaken to order his life.

Two principles were chosen by Rosmini early in life as the foundation of all that he wished to accomplish.[72]

1) To think seriously about correcting my enormous vices and purifying my soul from the evil which weighs it down from birth, without looking for other occupations or undertakings on behalf of my neighbour (I see that it is completely impossible for me to do anything of myself to my neighbour's advantage);

2) not to refuse any duties of charity towards my neighbour when divine Providence offers and presents them to me (God can use anyone, even me, to accomplish his works), to remain completely open to all works of charity, doing what God offers me — as far as my free will is concerned — with as much devotion as any other work.[73]

The insight leading to the formulation of these principles also showed him that the Christian life, the life of Christ within the spirit, is a call to the perfection of love. Only love can perfect the human person,[74] and only divine love can perfect the image and likeness of God that is found in the human person. God's work is central, therefore, to the Christian undertaking; the Christian's work lies in turning away from everything within himself that could impede God's work.

The paradox is expressed in words which, although strange and contradictory at first sight, indicate with the utmost clarity what has to be done by God and the Christian as the inner life unfolds:

[72] Cf. pp. 2-3.
[73] *Vita*, vol. 1, pp. 208-209.
[74] Cf. p. 17.

Hence the Christian's desire and endeavour to be borne with all the longings and actions of his life totally into God, in so far as this is possible on earth, in accordance with the obligation imposed on him: 'You shall love the Lord your God with all your heart, and with all your soul, and with all your mind', and 'You shall love your neighbour as yourself.'[75]

'Desiring to be borne' indicates the activity and the passivity requisite in the Christian life, and it is deliberately reminiscent of words which describe God's loving action towards his chosen ones: 'You have seen ... how I bore you on eagles' wings and brought you to myself' (Ex 19: 4).

The best means for achieving this end common to all Christians is the following of Christ according to the profession of 'effective poverty, chastity and obedience.'[76] This kind of discipleship, when undertaken by several people together for the sake of 'mutual help and encouragement'[77] constitutes the state or way called 'religious life', which itself must be practised for 'the purpose of increasing the perfection of love to which all [their] fellow-Christians are likewise called'. This was Rosmini's calling, to which he was faithful all his life.

But Rosmini enlarges on the nature of the end common to Christians by showing how it implies the single desire of union with Christ in God and of thus pleasing God.

The Christian's aim is to become one with Jesus as closely as Jesus is one with the Father. His desire must be insatiable, and he must never be afraid of asking too much.[78]

The desire, unlimited and measureless, 'must be rendered pure and most sincere in the disciple', whoever he may be. Rosmini goes on, with words which lift the veil slightly on his own deep spirit of prayer, to describe how this is to be done:

He [the Christian] can obtain this by constantly repeating [the desire], concentrated within himself and withdrawn from all external things to a perfect inner solitude, where he must

[75] *MP*, lesson 1, no. 2.

[76] *MP*, lesson 1, no. 3.

[77] Const. no. 2.

[78] *MP*, lesson 2, no. 3.

persevere with the same request: 'Watch at all times, praying'(Lk 21: 36).[79]

The difficulties experienced in achieving this interior solitude — sin, selfishness, anxiety about inward and outward circumstances — are not unknown to Rosmini, but the Christian, the new person redeemed by Christ and possessing his Spirit

> must not be in the least dismayed, nor hold back, if external things do make an impression on him. When this happens he must recollect himself once more, and in the solitude of his heart ceaselessly renew his desire ... until he longs for nothing on earth unless it leads to ... the perfect fulfilment of whatever is most pleasing to God.[80]

The single-mindedness of this desire does not, however, make the Christian turn in upon himself:

> This fundamental longing ... implies all possible good desires, so that he who possesses this great desire desires the salvation of all his fellows in the way pleasing to God, and willed by God.[81]

The end which the Christian must make his own is given more concrete application by Rosmini as he shows what is implied in the 'great desire'. The Christian who wants all possible glory for God

> longs for everything whatsoever that God holds dear. Now the Christian knows by faith that our heavenly Father finds all his satisfaction in Jesus Christ, his only-begotten Son, and that Jesus Christ, the only-begotten Son, finds his satisfaction in the faithful who form his kingdom. The Christian, therefore, can never be mistaken when he takes the entire *holy Church* as the object of his affections, thoughts, desires and actions. He knows for certain what God wants in the Church's regard, and is sure that, in accordance with the divine will, the Church of Jesus Christ is the great means through which God's holy name is to be fully glorified.[82]

Within 'the entire holy Church, ... the immaculate Bride of

[79] *MP*, lesson 2, no. 6.
[80] *MP*, lesson 2, no. 7.
[81] *MP*, lesson 2, no. 10.
[82] *MP*, lesson 3, no. 2.

Jesus Christ,' there is one essential part on earth — the rock, 'St. Peter, the head of the Apostles, and his successors, the bishops of Rome, supreme vicars of Jesus Christ on earth.'[83] The Christian's love for this part of the Church on earth 'must be without limit, and in every way he must endeavour to further its genuine holiness, glory, renown and prosperity.'[84] As he lives out his life in this way, however, he suffers no anxiety. Jesus Christ alone

> guides all events, directing them by his wisdom, power and incomparable goodness according to his divine good pleasure for the greater good of the persons he has chosen to form his beloved Bride, the Church. The Christian, therefore, relying entirely on his Lord, will be perfectly tranquil and content.[85]

In the light of this truth concerning Jesus' unfailing direction of his Church, Rosmini was able to jot down at 17 years of age:

> Some of these thoughts have been written by a youth who has not yet studied philosophy, but described what his reason offered him as new and beautiful. He wants to note, however, that he is always subject to the Church, that is, to the truth, and always ready to retract whatever he has written that is not approved by her.[86]

He repeated the same concept many years later when storms were beginning to blow up around him:

> I was not born to be learned or to gain glory from human beings, nor have I ever aimed at this in my poor labours. I was born to be a believer and made worthy of the promises of Christ, as a devout son of the Church ... My treasure is the holy faith, and here my heart is to be found also. If it should happen, let us say, that the holy apostolic See, my teacher and the teacher of the whole world, were to find something to correct in my works, I would have no difficulty in making any public declaration that could render my unshaken faith more clear. Anything I could have said against this faith, I would

[83] *MP*, lesson 3, no. 10.
[84] *Ibid*.
[85] *MP*, lesson 4, no. 1.
[86] *Vita*, vol. 1, p. 67.

certainly have maintained against my own feeling for things.
Retracting what I had said would simply mean expressing the
unchangeable thought I held in my heart, and correcting its
external expression which would have failed to render exactly
my intimate conviction — that is, my faith ... All my trust is
in God alone who infused me with faith as a baby and gave
me an unlimited devotion to the decisions of the Holy See. He
fills my heart with joy when I can make an act of faith, and
would almost make me glad to have fallen into some involuntary error, without damaging others, in order to be able to
confess my faith more deeply and solemnly.'[87]

We may turn now to Rosmini, the spiritual person rather
than the spiritual writer, as he journeys from Gaeta to his
brethren at Stresa. His mission has been a failure, and his work
for the Church discounted at the Papal court; he has suffered
genuine humiliation. But as far as he knows, Pius IX is not
displeased with him. Rosmini is completely unaware of the
prohibition of his two works which, written solely for love of
the Church, are an expression of his deep and lasting love for
the Papacy, a love in which he sees an essential outlet for his
love of God and neighbour. The *Five Wounds of the Church* in
particular is intended simply 'to point to the agony of the Church'
and 'to illustrate more clearly the sorrows which now afflict [her].'

Rosmini was studying in the library of the diocesan seminary of Albano, near Rome, when he received news of the
intended prohibition in a letter brought to him from the
Master of the Apostolic Palace. He was asked whether it was
his intention to submit to the decree. Within half an hour the
bearer of the letter left the seminary with the reply:

By the grace of God, I have always been at heart, and publicly
professed myself to be a most devoted and obedient child of
the Holy See. As such, I declare that I submit to the prohibition of the named books purely, simply and in every best way
possible. And I beg you to assure our most Holy Father and
the sacred Congregation of this.[88]

[87] to Don Paolo Bertolozzi, *EC.*, vol. 7, p. 616.

[88] to Padre Buttaoni, Master of the Sacred Palace, *EC.*, vol. 10, p.
586.

Rosmini, the spiritual person, was no less true to his principles in practice than Rosmini, the spiritual writer, was clear in enunciating them.

Other letters of this period mirror his interior attitude:

This unexpected event [the prohibition of his two books] has not altered in any way my peace and tranquillity of spirit. Rather, I have been able to offer sincere feelings of gratitude and praise to divine Providence which disposes everything for love, and has permitted this for love alone. But this tranquillity is not something that can be called my own. I would be a prey to every kind of disturbance and passion if he who hears our humble prayers and knows what we need in our weakness had not mercifully protected me with his grace, and put his own divine order in place of my disorder.[89]

Again:

If this [the prohibition] is counted a dishonour amongst men who judge that I have been guilty of some grave defect, we should remember that we must be disposed to follow Jesus Christ equally *sive per infamiam, sive per bonam famam* (in ill repute and good repute). So let us be glad and rejoice if we are humiliated and allowed to suffer something in imitation of Jesus Christ.[90]

And he wrote:

Thank you for sharing in the strange and almost incredible events through which I am being led by Providence whose unchanging design never fails. Meditating on Providence, I wonder at it; wondering at it, I love it; loving it, I celebrate it; celebrating it, I thank it, and thanking it I am filled with joy. Could it be otherwise? I know through reason and through faith, and feel in the depths of my spirit, that everything done, or wished or permitted by God, is done by eternal, infinite, essential Love. And who could be sad before love?[91]

It is clear from these extracts from his letters that Rosmini practised what he preached about commitment to the Church for love of God. But he came to these heights of sanctity

---

[89] to Don Paolo Barola, *EC.*, vol. 10, p. 599.
[90] to Don Giacomo Molinari, *EC.*, vol. 10, p. 600.
[91] to Don Michele Parma, *EC.*, vol. 10, p. 603.

through his grace-given willingness to abandon himself wholly to the care of divine Providence, to acknowledge profoundly his own nothingness and to direct all the actions of his life with what he calls 'a spirit of intelligence', 'which will certainly lead the Christian to attend to his own amendment first, before that of his neighbour'. The man who had entered upon his maturity by praying: 'Father, as your Son would pray in me, so I would pray', is now able to live a life of complete abandonment, showing through his own example the truth of what he had written as a young priest:

> To abandon oneself wholly to the care of divine Providence.
> — There is perhaps no maxim which helps more than this to obtain the peace of heart and stability of mind proper to the Christian life.
> This maxim, if practised with the simplicity and generosity of heart that it requires, excels perhaps all others in making the follower of Jesus Christ pleasing to his heavenly Father. For it implies absolute confidence in the Father and in him alone, together with complete independence of everything on earth that appears to offer gratification, power or fame; it implies a tender love reserved for God alone; it implies a living faith, enabling the Christian to hold without doubt that all things in the world, great and small, are in the hands of our heavenly Father and operate only as he disposes for the accomplishment of his wonderful plans. Through this faith the Christian trusts in the infinite goodness, mercy, munificence and generosity of his heavenly Father who in everything works for the good of those who trust in him, and whose gifts, favours, graces and care are in proportion to the confidence his beloved children place in him.[92]

At the end of his laborious, painful and strangely peaceful life, Rosmini as he lay dying was able to comfort and reassure Manzoni when the great writer spoke of his concern that Rosmini's death would deprive the world of someone who was so needed. 'What shall we do without you?' he asked Rosmini. The man of faith encapsulated the practice of a lifetime and summarised the counsel he had constantly

[92] *MP*, lesson 5, no. 2.

given to others with the sublime words: 'Adore, be silent and rejoice'.[93]

He died at Stresa, on the Lago Maggiore in northern Italy, on July 1st 1855.

[93] *Vita*, vol. 2, p. 505.